Sad Papaw
The Early Years

Kenneth Harmon

Charlotte Hopkins

MERRY CHRISTMAS

To SISTER RuBy

Kenny (SAD PAPAW) Harmon

Dedication

This book is dedicated to Wanda Perrin Harmon and John Edwin Harmon. With special thanks to Pruitt Lewis and Joe Bailey Lewis

Acknowledgments

To Richard Boyd, Secretary for the Oklahoma Law Enforcement Museum & Hall of Fame. And to Wesley Horton, founder of the American Institute of Drive-In Archaeology.

Table Of Contents

Page 1   The Making of Sad Papaw

Page 20   Family Life in the Sooner State

Page 56   Harmon Family Farming Years

Page 71   Church Days

Page 76   A Sweeter Side of Kenny's World

Page 93   Oklahoma Lawmen

Page 128   Growing Up In Oklahoma

Page 159   Tragedy on the Homefront

Page 162   Celebrating 47

Preface

With one single tweet from a teenage girl about having burgers with her grandfather and a wave of empathy for grandparents everywhere swept around the world. After realizing the impact that single message made, Kenny Harmon extended his gratitude by hosting a community cookout that everyone was invited to. And supporters came in droves from his neighboring communities of Oklahoma to as far away as Australia. Many have been left wondering ~ what happened to Sad Papaw. Not only is he letting his fans get caught up on the changes that have happened to him since the cookout, he is sharing with the rest of us short stories of his own grandparents. From the days that he was called Baby Quify to today as we know him to be ~ Sad Papaw, this is the story of the man, the myth, and the burgers.

The Tweet heard around the world!

Chapter One

The Making of Sad Papaw

One common theme that flows through the pages of the books detailing the lives of the Harmons is the importance of family. Kenny Harmon instilled this value into his children and then to his grandchildren, who stole his heart the minute he laid eyes on them. So, when he found out that his granddaughter Kelsey, who had been away at college, was home for a few days he planned a last-minute cookout. He invited Kelsey and the rest of his grandchildren over and went to work preparing burgers and home fries. Kelsey was the first to arrive. As the two chatted, Kenny continued to grill. As he finished cooking, they assembled their burgers and sat down with a hot plate of home fries. They also realized that none of the other grandchildren were coming that night. Kelsey decided to rub it into her cousins that they were missing out on the cookout. She grabbed her phone and snapped a picture of Kenny, with a somber look on his face, taking the first bite of his burger. She shared the photo on Twitter with the caption: "dinner with papaw tonight...he made 12 burgers for all 6 grandkids and I'm the only one who showed. love him."

This was simply to poke at her brother and her cousins for not showing up for the barbecue. Though minutes later, her brother, Kaleb, did arrive and joined them. Not thinking of the harmless picture that she had just taken, the three of them carried on with their meal. While they finished their burgers, the innocent tweet meant to tease her cousins was quickly spreading across the country – and soon, around the world. Hearts were breaking across the internet as Kenny's photo was shared. By morning, Kenny was internet famous and gained thousands of "new grandchildren."

The next day, Kenny was still unaware of the picture that was still surfing the web. That was until approximately, 3:00 in the afternoon, when his daughter, Abby, called him from her home in Garden Valley, California. He could hear laughter in the background and all Abby could mutter was "Hey Dad," until she too burst into laughter. Finally, she blurted out, "You need to call Ellen," and then she hung up the phone. He laughed and brushed it off, then continued his day. Two hours later, his son, Ryan, called him. The conversation started a lot like Abby's because he too was laughing (with more laughter in the background).

Ryan stated, "You need to call Ellen."

"What are you talking about? That's exactly what Abby said."

"You are all over the internet."

"Yeah right!" Kenny now believed this was some kind of joke.

He thought whatever it was it would go away. He would not even look at anything on the internet. The next morning on Friday, March 18th, Kenny was leaving to go to Pauls Valley to watch the Washington Warriors compete in a baseball game. His grandsons Brody and Brandon attended Washington High School and played on the team. Again, he got a call from Garden Valley, California. This time it was Rhonda, his ex-wife, of 40 years.

"I hope it's okay, I gave your number to someone."

"That's okay, who wanted to know?"

"Inside Edition."

"Okay, then it's true something is on the internet. Abby and Ryan called yesterday but I didn't believe the story."

Fifteen minutes after they talked, Inside Edition did indeed call, asking for an interview. There was no time to talk though, Kenny wanted to be at the baseball game (again showing, that with the Harmons, it is family first). He told them that he would be home in three hours. But the show was adamant that they talk to him sooner. They wanted to include his story on their afternoon show. At the time, Kenny did not have a iPhone. They asked if someone at the game might have a cell phone that he could use. He knew his grandsons both have phones and he knew that one of them would let him use their phone. His grandson, Brock, was also at the game and he let Kenny use his phone. They interviewed him from Paul Valley High School and that afternoon his interview was aired nationally. This was less than 48 hours after Kelsey's tweet.

People magazine also interviewed Kenny. He stated emphatically, "I don't have an iPhone or a Facebook and I don't do Social Media. So this could have gone on and on and I'd never know about it." That has since changed. He was also interviewed on Good Morning America and featured on Daily Mail and Buzz Feed.

All the while, the internet continued to spiral into a whirlwind of mixed emotions. Though the internet adored the man, now deemed Sad Papaw, they were furious with his grandchildren. Were these children really ungrateful to have this sweet man as their grandfather? Not exactly! In fact, that would not describe them at all. What the world did not know is that his failed cookout, as they knew it to be, was just a string of misunderstandings. The four grandchildren that did not show up for the cookout were Brock, Brody, Brandon, and Bryn. When Kenny called their dad, Ryan, that morning to invite them over he was extremely busy at work. By the time he made it home, the cookout simply slipped his mind. There was no malice or disrespect meant by that. Kelsey's brother, Kaleb, would get it the worst from Sad Papaw's new angry grandchildren. Kelsey and Kenny tried to explain that Kaleb actually was at the cookout but he showed up shortly after the tweet was released, that he did not even know about the tweet. They explained that Kaleb would never purposely hurt his grandfather. However, no matter how many times they echoed those words, no one would listen.

As the days went by, thousands of Sad Papaw fans reached out to console him. They also continued to unleash their anger for his grandchildren. Some created memes to poke fun at the situation but others actually started sending death threats to the grandchildren that did not show. Everything happened so fast and left Kenny feeling bittersweet. On one hand, he wanted to reach back to those who showed concern. On the other hand, he wanted to protect his grandchildren, to make peace and rein in the anger. The family talked about what to do and Brock had the idea for an open cookout. A huge picnic that would be open to the public. They could share a burger with Papaw like so many showed interest in doing. The grandchildren took to Facebook and Twitter to announce that social media's favorite grandfather was having a cookout in Purcell at the family's flea market and everyone was invited. Kenny predicted that there might be 150 – 200 people at the cookout. Brock thought otherwise, telling Kenny that if half the people showed up that said they would, then there would be closer to 2,000 guests.

After a week of planning the cookout, the big day arrived. Saturday, March 26th, was a warm and toasty day. Papaw's legendary burgers were sizzling on the grill and Sad Papaw was ready for his meet & greet. There were t-shirts and hats laid out for sale so visitors could take home a souvenir proclaiming they "ate a burger with Sad Papaw." As travelers arrived throughout the day, a line stretched 40 yards long. The cookout started at 10 AM and Kenny spent the first hour running the grill. As more and more people showed up, his son took over the cooking so that Kenny could meet his supporters. For six hours Kenny met the most amazing Sad Papaw boosters (and boost they did)!! A man from Texas expressed to reporters, "I don't have a Paw Paw. All my family's passed away, so I want to show him my support." Another of Sad Papaw's guests stated, "It's totally like an American thing and I was just like, 'Nah I can't miss it.'" She lives in Australia but was in California doing business at the time of the cookout. Sharon Fernandez, who also traveled from California with her daughters, shared with a KWTV reporter, that it was seeing Kenny's sad face that motivated her to make the 20-hour drive to Sad Papaw's cookout. "It was sad, you know? Here he makes this dinner for his grandchildren, but I understand it, we all have busy lives."

In the end, over 2,000 people attended the cookout to have a burger with Sad Papaw. They served more than 1,700 burgers. Kenny was thankful that Brock stepped up and said to plan for more than 200 because they increased their order of products by 1,000 – and they still ran short. They had to take a quick trip to the store for more hamburger meat, drinks, and picnic supplies. Along with the family from Australia, there were people from Canada, Hong Kong, and Germany. There were 28 states represented at the cookout, including Texas, Oregon, Indiana, Missouri, Nevada, Arkansas, Pennsylvania, Minnesota, Colorado, California, New Hampshire, Illinois, Washington, New York, Florida, North Carolina, Maryland, Mississippi, Louisiana, Arizona, South Dakota, Kansas, Iowa, Michigan, Georgia, South Carolina, Virginia, and Ohio. There were four more amazing teens that stepped up to the plate that day to help things go smoothly. Drake Harmon (Kenny's adopted son), Colton Hager (Larry Hager's grandson), and family friends Nathan and Austin Malchaski. They parked and retrieved cars across 2 1/2 acres of land. They spent the day walking, jogging, and running back & forth to help people. The most ironic part of the day's events was that Kelsey, the Harmon who started the Sad Papaw craze, was not at this cookout. She had a college softball game so she could not attend. The other five grandchildren not only attended the cookout, they worked on the grill and helped serve food from start to finish. America's saddest grandfather was all-smiles at the end of the day.

Kenny took photos with his guests and listened wholeheartedly and at times fought back tears as he listened to guests share stories of their own grandfathers. They expressed their own regret over missing the opportunities to spend time with their grandfathers and most importantly to tell them how much they love them. Kenny and his family hoped that the outpouring of loved that was shown to their family will also lead visitors and online friends to value their own grandparents. Brock Harmon told KWTV, "If you've got your grandparents, go see them. Take them to dinner. Go hang out. Realize they're not going to be around forever." It was a long day but it was not over yet. A 3-man crew from Inside Edition came to his house for more photos and interviews. That lasted approximately 45 minutes. He was ready to call it a day!

There were two more endearing highlights that grew from the events stemming back to Kelsey's tweet. The first was a gift from Alegiant Airlines. They presented Kenny with 13 tickets to an all expense paid vacation to Destin, Florida. They spent the week staying in a 3-story condo, which was a seven bedroom beach house. Kenny did not forget the contributions from Drake, Colton, Nathan, and Austin, who spent 6 hours parking cars in the hot sun. He paid for 4 extra tickets to the Destin beach trip to reward them for their kindness and hard work. Kenny told Wear TV, "We have never had a vacation like this with this many of our family. We've had vacations with a few of the grandkids but we've never had a vacation like this with our grandkids. This is really special."

The second highlight came in the form of friendship. Kenny now had friends around the world. One, in particular, was Abby Hensley. She is a cashier who works at Spencer's Grocery in Blanchard. He was shopping one day and standing in Abby's line, behind an elderly woman. Abby looked up at him and said, "Awe, you got a Sad Papaw shirt." Then she paused when she realized WHO she was talking to. Then she stated, "You ARE Sad Papaw!" She stopped what she was doing to come around the counter to give him a hug and take her picture with him. They are still friends today.

The tweet that started an internet frenzy of anger, awareness, and compassion ended in a way that continues to make Kenny proud. It brought awareness to the importance of acknowledging our grandparents. Loving them and spending as much time as possible with them. Appreciating our grandparents is a message that many fail to grasp until it's too late. Now, thanks to Kenny and Kelsey Harmon, thousands of grandparents were surprised by visits from their own grandchildren. The day of Kenny's cookout one of his supporters posted on his Facebook page that she and her children packed up their car and were driving to meet him and decided to turn around and go back to her own grandfather's house to surprise him with a visit and their own impromptu cookout. It is moments like that, for Kenny, that make this Sad Papaw, one happy man!

Author Notes: Kenny Harmon continues to host community cookouts that are dedicated to American Vets (who eat for free).

danielle ward @**do_well_do_good_**

Totally reasonable journey for a burger with Papaw!! i'm coming!!

Images from Sad Papaw's world famous cookout!

Everyone had a great time!

Two of Papaw's children, a few of his grandkids, along with some of their friends. They all joined Papaw on his trip to Destin, Florida.

Sad Papaw's Supporters Have Their Chance to Take to Twitter

Courtney McDonald @courtney6379 · 4h

Papaw.... @papaw

LarryFI$herman
@charlesjonesss

⚙ &+ Follow

Idk what was cookin better the burgers or me n papaw in these pics 😎 🍔 💯

RETWEETS 20   LIKES 75

4:47 PM - 26 Mar 2016

👤 Ben Dykes

Papaw's cookout was a success

RETWEETS LIKES
10   75

4:36 PM - 26 Mar 2016

Mario Marquez
@mariombe   Follow

We also ate a burger with sad papaw
#sadnomore #papawcookout #roadtrip
@Mayola_leal

 **Victoria Bumgarner**
@vickybumgarner

 ⚙ + Follow

The line for #papawcookout is insane! So much love for Papaw! #Oklahoma

RETWEETS   LIKES
373   675

1:30 PM · 26 Mar 2016

Oklahoma, USA

 amber pitcher @ambalamb95 · 7h
I ate a burger with sad papaw
@BHarmon_10

♻ 2   ♥ 18

Independent Ents ✓
@IndoEnts

⚙ ⚲ Follow

Remember Sad Papaw? He threw a cookout
and more than 1500 people came.
indo.ie/ZY1xX #papawcookout

RETWEET LIKES
1   2

1:00 PM - 27 Mar 2016

Rini
@rini_the_ripper

⚙ ⚲ Follow

Enjoyed a delicious burger with #SadPapaw at
the #papawcookout You have a great family
@_papaw_

RETWEETS LIKES
6   18

7:40 PM - 26 Mar 2016

Campbell Flemmons
@Campbell_McCall

Follow

We had burgers with Papaw #papawcookout #oklahoma #vip

RETWEETS 19   LIKES 56

10:09 PM · 26 Mar 2016

281 - 330 - 8004
@___colshearted

Follow

We had a BLAST at Papaws cookout today in Purcell, Oklahoma 🍔🐄💕 #SadPapaw #papawcookout #burgerswithpapaw

RETWEETS 3   LIKES 9

9:46 PM · 26 Mar 2016

 **Taylor Brady Lee**
@TaylorBrady101

So glad I had the opportunity to eat a burger
with #papaw at the #papawcookout now back
to MS.

RETWEETS   LIKES
2   11

6:23 PM - 26 Mar 2016

Chapter 2

Family Life in the Sooner State

The 1940's and 1950's brought on a world of changes in America. Morton salt now had a place on kitchen tables. M&M's were created by Forrest Mars Sr. and Bruce Murrie, the son of the Hershey candy company. The candy was specifically made as a chocolate treat that can be carried by US troops entering the war. Aerosol cans were lining store shelves in a variety of products. To the delight of children (and some adults), Superman debuted in movie theaters. The JEEP rolled off the assembly lines. Michigan led the way of adding fluoride to the public water supply after it was discovered that fluoride can fight tooth decay. The long-playing (LP) record was first made. It was favored because it was a record that could hold more than 1 song. More fun and convenient products introduced to the public were the electric blankets, Elmer's glue, silly putty, the slinky, and the Polaroid instant camera. One of the biggest breakthroughs was in the field of medicine, with Alexander Fleming's invention of Penicillin. The discovery would herald the way for a number of antibiotics that followed.

Changes were churning and changing the lives of families in Oklahoma. Three years earlier, in 1937, the small town of Dibble, Oklahoma was incorporated and named after James and John Dibble. Before that, Dibble was a small part of Chickasaw. In this small town of Dibble, with less than 100 residents, lived two hardworking families, the Perrins and the Harmons. Wanda Perrin was a soft-spoken teen who was a popular student at Dibble High School. She met Billy Harmon on the school bus they both rode every day. He was an outgoing athlete in school but when it came to the girls, he was more on the shy side. Billy and Wanda quickly became friends. From there it grew into a love that would expand the decades. If you ask Billy he will tell you that, for him, it was love at first sight. In the Harmon family, this was a monumental year. For it was exactly, 100 years before Billy and Wanda met and fell in love, that Billy's ancestors, Peter Harman and Mary Creekmore met and fell in love. A beautiful tribute to the growing Harmon family. Wanda and Billy dated throughout high school, including attending prom together. Billy was two years older than Wanda so he graduated first but their relationship stayed strong.

One week before Wanda was to graduate Billy asked her to marry him. But the wedding...well, that did not go as well as they thought it would. One Friday afternoon the couple traveled to a nearby courthouse and were married by the Justice of Peace. However, after Billy kissed the bride, they were told the marriage would not be legal because Wanda was underage. She would need a written letter of consent from her parents. And it had to be notarized. So, the race was on to get back to Wanda's house, get a letter written and make it to the notary, all of this before their offices closed. They made it back to Wanda's house and informed her parents what they had done, just in time for the office doors at the Notary's office to close for the night. Saturday morning, along with Wanda's mother, and a consent letter in hand they had the letter notarized. Now the tricky part was, where can they get married on a Saturday morning? Everything was closed. But Wanda and Billy were determined! First, they went to the Sheriff's office, hoping he could wed the couple. He could not do it. But he was able to track down a judge who met them at the Justice of the Peace office, on the second floor of the bank building. The sheriff unlocked the doors and the two, once again took their vows. On May 22, 1948, after two days – and two weddings - they were officially husband and wife.

There was no honeymoon for the young couple but they did not care. They got what they wanted, which was to start their new life as husband and wife. That afternoon they moved in with Billy's parents. This would be a temporary stay while they got their own home ready. There were minor repairs to make, painting to be done, and furniture to gather.

A year after they were married, Wanda became pregnant with their first child. This was even more motivation to finish their first home. Just finding out that she was pregnant would be a somewhat long medical process. There were no sonogram machines. And no home pregnancy tests. Wanda went to the doctor's and had to give a urine sample, that was then sent away for testing. At the lab, the urine was injected into a rabbit. If the rabbit died that meant she was pregnant. Sure enough, on this day for Wanda – the rabbit died.

Wanda faced many do's and don'ts of being a mom. Though they were much more relaxed than the generations of women in her family before her. For starters, people now shuttered to say the words "pregnant" and "pregnancy" in public. Instead, they opted for more proper terms, such as, "expecting", "with child" and "in the family way." Smoking and drinking were allowed and even the doctor would offer the ladies a cigarette if they were nervous at their appointments. Hospital staff visited new parents to sell packs of cigarettes to them. Wanda was encouraged to have a great deal of bed rest, as much as possible, since she was now in a delicate stage. This was a far step from her ancestors who worked on the farm or in the garden until the day they went into labor.

Wanda was also advised not to reach for things overhead because it was believed that she would wrap the umbilical cord around the baby's neck. In fact, if the umbilical cord was wrapped around the baby's neck she knew she would be accused of being too active or reaching for something.

It was winter in the last few months of her pregnancy and she was warned by her doctor (and the women in her family) not to sit on cold concrete because she could get hemorrhoids that way. She was also told to brush her teeth often to keep from getting morning sickness.

Wanda was warned by her doctor to gain only between 16-20 pounds. If Wanda came close to going over that she would be put on a diet and given pills to lose weight, and keep it down. At that time, some women were given pills called Dexedrine. It would later be discovered that Dexedrine caused babies to be born with birth defects and missing limbs. However, that same medication would later be used to treat ADHD. She was also told that it would be perfectly acceptable for her to smoke cigarettes to keep her pregnancy weight down to a minimum. In fact, hospital rooms in the Maternity Ward had ashtrays in them.

As Wanda's due date approached, the doctor had a few suggestions to help bring on her labor. One way was to take a few teaspoons of orange juice and castor oil every day. Billy and Wanda were told to take rides on a bumpy road. They believed the continuous bumps would shake the baby and push him to come out from his mother's belly.

Preparing for the baby also meant getting a crib, a wooden playpen, with spinner toys on the side, a pram, safety pins, and stacks of nappies (cloth diapers). The baby would need 10-12 nappies a day (at least). They would need to be washed thoroughly between diaper changes which made laundry seem like a never-ending task.

The fun part of preparing for the baby was picking a name! Billy and Wanda tossed around a few ideas. They were determined to name their first baby after someone – but who? The name they chose for a boy was Kenneth Layne. The name "Kenneth" came from Billy's brother, Ken. He was given his middle name "Layne" from Lester Lane, a local popular athlete. Oklahoma was always a state that admired their sports players. They did not have a major league basketball team so they followed the college leagues instead. In 1949, a few months before Kenny was born, Lester Layne was becoming a household name for sports fans in Oklahoma.

In that same year, Oklahoma's up-and-coming star, Lester Lane, was a senior at Purcell High School and already a household name – as a rising star in sports! Lane grew up in Purcell, the neighboring community of Dibble. After he graduated, Lane went on to the University of Oklahoma. There he competed in pole vaulting for the Sooner track team. He also played basketball and football. In basketball, he scored 1,180 points. It was a record that would not be broken for 11 years. He won the gold medal in the 1960 Olympics and was one of the shortest basketball players to ever play in the Olympic games. His roommate at the Olympics was Oscar Robertson, who went on to have a great career in the NBA playing for the Cincinnati Royals and the Milwaukee Bucks. After Lane's death in 1973, the town renamed the Fourth Street, in his name – Lester Lane. It is located just south of Main Street. The Harmons were hardcore sports fans. They were honored to name their son after Lester Lane.

Less than two weeks after ringing in the new year, their big day arrived. Wanda was in labor. As soon as they reached the hospital, Billy and Wanda were separated as she was taken in the back to give birth. Billy waited nervously in the waiting room. He was soon joined by Wanda's family and members of his own family. Wanda was taken to a small, dimly-lit room where she waited with a nurse while the labor progressed. There was little interaction between Wanda and the nurses. She was pretty much alone to struggle through her labor pains. However, there were five other women in the room with her. Their beds were lined up side-by-side.

When the pain got to be too much they gave her a shot to put her to sleep. That is where it gets dangerous for Wanda and the baby. The state they were putting her in was called Twilight Sleep. The shot they gave her was a combination of morphine (to provide pain relief) and scopolamine (basically, to wipe away any memory of the event). The side effects included Wanda thrashing about in her sleep state. A few hours later Wanda woke up to see a nurse standing over her, asking if she would like to hold her new baby boy. On Thursday, January 12, 1950, their son, Kenneth Layne Harmon was born. It was on that day that Billy and Wanda truly felt like a family.

Billy would still have a little longer to wait to see his son. No one in the family was allowed to see Wanda or the baby until they were both washed up and thought to be presentable. After that, he and the family could only view Kenny through the glass window of the maternity ward. Wanda was not allowed to hold the baby for 24 hours after giving birth because the medication used in her labor could cause her to drop the baby.

During Wanda's stay in the hospital, she was only allowed to see her baby during feeding time. No one, including Billy, was allowed in the room during feeding time. In the hospital, she bottle fed her baby but once at home she would breastfeed. For most new moms, like Wanda, breastfeeding was expected. If they failed for any reason, then the baby was put on either Similac or Carnation milk. There was no education from the hospital staff on how to breastfeed. Women were mostly left on their own to learn from trial and error. In fact, the only instruction Wanda was given was to only feed him for a half hour, every 4 hours and if he cries in between feedings to give him bottles of water. If she was unable to breastfeed it would be said that she was doing something wrong. Sadly, that often left women feeling like they were failures as mothers if they could not breastfeed. Wanda was also told, by the other women in her family, to remain calm when she was breastfeeding. They told her if she was angry or aggravated at all she could cause Kenny to get colic.

A week after Wanda gave birth, she and Kenny were allowed to go home. Being that there were no car seats, (that would not happen until 1962), Wanda carried her baby on her lap on the drive home. She did this often when they needed to go places. Or Kenny would be put in a basket on the back seat.

Most people waited, at least, a month before they came to the Harmon home to see the new baby. Having him baptized was also important. In fact, most parents did not let their new baby leave the house until the day of their baptism.

When Kenny was 4 months old, Wanda gave him his first tastes of food. This included rice pudding and even a small serving of boiled tripe. Tripe is the stomach lining from the cow, pig, or sheep. It was believed to be the best thing for Kenny because it was high in iron.

Wanda received parenting tips from friends and family that differed greatly from advice received by ancestors before her (and the ones that followed after her). She was told not to rock Kenny often or jostle him because this would cause him to be too stimulated and he would not sleep. So she only rocked him when it was necessary, which was usually just briefly before he fell asleep. Kenny was expected to sleep up to 20 hours a day in the first month and if he did not get that much sleep then it was said that Wanda was doing something wrong. Any parenting techniques that did not work out well were blamed on Wanda.

When Kenny cried Wanda tried her best not to coddle him and to just leave him alone. She and Billy were told that crying was great exercise for his lungs. If his lungs did not get enough exercise then they could collapse. Her doctor told her it would be perfectly safe to leave him outside in his pram if she did not want to hear him cry anymore.

There were no parenting classes or any resources for education. All parents had to go on to educate themselves – besides advice from families – were a few parenting books. The first one was "Common Sense in the Nursery." It was published by Mrs. Frankenburg in 1922 (later revised in 1934 and 1954). She was the first to stress that their lungs would not expand to their fullest extent unless they were allowed to exercise them daily. Frankenburg went on to say, "If nature is regularly thwarted by some well-meaning person who picks up the baby and distracts his attention after the first squeak, there is a risk of the lungs remaining almost unexpanded." To support her argument she cited the case of an 8-month-old baby who died of pneumonia, claiming the main cause was his parents coddling him instead of allowing him to cry which made his lungs weak.

In 1939 Mary Stopes wrote, Your Baby's First Year." It was on her advice that parents believed that their newborn should sleep up to 22 hours a day in the first month. From the 3rd to the 5th month, they can let them sleep for 20 hours a day. From the 7th month until the age of one they should sleep 18 hours a day. Stopes also confirmed Mrs. Frankenburg's opinion that babies should be allowed to cry to strengthen their lungs. However, she also warned not to overdo it, that some coddling was safe.

Things got a little risky when he started crawling and reaching for things. There was no baby proofing. Billy and Wanda were expected to simply train him the strict way, of what to touch and what was "Mommy's stuff."

The day Kenny was born it was chilly and raining. In fact, it rained almost every day that month. Kenny was often lulled to sleep by the sound of rain on the rooftop. There was a total of 9" of rain that fell that month. That's quite a lot when you consider that 1" of rain is equal to 10" of snow. When he turned 6 months old, he was starting to crawl. He just got his feel of the grass, flowers, and dirt at his feet when along came more rain, pounding Dibble harder than ever. It was the rainiest July that Dibble would experience throughout the entire 1900's.

The following year was rough on Oklahoma. After just surviving one of their rainiest seasons, tornadoes touched down in Dibble, Oklahoma for the first time. The first was on Monday, February 19, 1951. Two F2 tornadoes swept through Dibble on Monday, April 5, 1951. April was not safe yet, still, another tornado approached. An F3 tornado touched down on Monday, April 30th. The last tornado of 1951 came through on Wednesday, June 6th. Fortunately, the Harmons and the Perrins survived them all, unscathed.

The year Kenny was born, the country was at war against North Korea. Which brought the draft in full motion. The friction in Korea began in 1948 when the north and south divided into their own regions, with their own governments and laws. Each proclaimed to be the correct government to rule over Korea. Neither would acknowledge the border that was an unwritten rule between the two. This brought on a number of clashes between the north and south, alongside the country's border. It all escalated on June 25, 1950, when North Korea stormed across the border and invaded the south. America was one of 16 countries that came to the aid of South Korea, sending troops, equipment, and assistance. China and the USSR came to the aid of North Korea.

The state of Oklahoma participated in the war in a variety of ways. Tinker Air Force Base in Oklahoma City provided maintenance for bombers and cargo planes. The U.S. Army Field Artillery at Fort Sill, Oklahoma trained soldiers preparing to enter the war. What most people do not know is that Chickasha, Oklahoma also housed two Prison of War (POW) Internment Camps. They first opened during World War II. Oklahoma was chosen because of the mild temperatures and the access to a large number of farms that could be used to put prisoners to work. The POW camps were located at Camp Gruber at Muskogee, Fort McAlester in the town McAlester. and Fort Sill at Lawton.

America's participation in the war ended on July 27, 1953. The fear of communists invading America was strong and companies made employees sign Loyalty Agreements, promising never to join any type of group that supported communism. Almost 40,000 Americans died in the war and over 100,000 more soldiers came home injured.

All of Oklahoma's Korean War Veterans are honorable in the eyes of their citizens. There is one Blanchard vet that seemed to stand out. His name was Tony Burris. He was a Sergeant First Class with the Army, a member of Company L, 38th Infantry Regiment. The wording on the Congressional Medal letter describes the events of the battle scene that led to his death on October 8, 1951.

"On 8 October, when his company encountered intense fire from a entrenched hostile force, Sergeant First Class Burris charged forward alone, throwing grenades into the position and destroying approximately fifteen of the enemy. On the following day, spearheading a renewed assault on enemy positions on the next ridge, he was assaulted by machine gun fire but continued the assault, reaching the crest of the ridge ahead of his unit and sustaining a second wound. Calling for a 57mm recoilless rifle team, he deliberately exposed himself to draw hostile fire and reveal the enemy position. The enemy machine gun emplacement was destroyed. The Company then moved forward and prepared to assault other positions on the ridge line. Sergeant First Class Burris refusing evacuation and submitting only to emergency treatment, joined the unit in its renewed attack but fire from hostile emplacements halted the advance. Sergeant First Class Burris rose to his feet, charged forward and destroyed the first emplacement with its heavy machine

gun and crew of six men. Moving out to the next emplacement, and throwing his last grenade which destroyed this position, he fell mortally wounded by enemy fire. Inspired by his consummate gallantry, his comrades renewed a spirited assault which overran enemy positions and secured Hill 605, a strategic position in the battle for "Heartbreak Ridge." Sergeant Tony K. Burris' indominable fighting spirit, outstanding heroism, and gallant self-sacrifice reflect the highest glory upon himself, the Infantry, and the United States Army."

Because of his heroism in the Korean War, his hometown, Blanchard, Oklahoma posted a statue in his honor, at the northeast corner of Second Street and N. Main. The large bronze statue is poised on a rock base. There are several plaques on the rock that describe his heroic service. One of the plaques is encrypted with the last letter that Burris wrote home to his family. It reads as followed.

"I received word from a pretty reliable source the other day that no one from our regiment will be rotated until this new attack is over with, so that will be just that much longer before it becomes my turn...it is so chilly at night—I would hate to spend another winter here. Love, Tony."

About 100 feet away from the statue is a war memorial with a marble stone with the words: "Freedom is not free – never has been, never will be. The veterans honored here knew that we will remain forever in their debt."

When Kenny was a year old their house was ready. The small home was directly up the hill from Billy's parents. Sadly, their happiness did not last long. Later that year, the family went out to a movie and came home to see that their house caught on fire while they were away and burned to the ground. They are not sure if the fire was started by a hot coal from the stove or from a kerosene lamp that was left on that night. A fire that took less than 12 minutes to swallow their home had taken everything the young couple owned. They were forced to move into an old potato house that was located on the edge of Babe and Nellie's yard. The small building was 40 feet long and 20 feet wide. There was no indoor carpeting but a concrete floor instead. They did not have an overhead ceiling, there was only a cement roof protecting them from the outside elements. The walls were made of a clay tile. They did have the benefit of electric lights, a 50-gallon barrel heater, refrigerator/ice box, and a cast iron stove. It may not sound like much but Wanda made it into a cozy home for her family. Even Kenny's cousin, Gayla Hollis, looks back on the potato house as being one of her favorite places to visit.

Their next move was to a 3-room house, that was nicknamed "the shack." Wanda was so happy to be back into a house that she did not seem to mind that it did not have running water or insulation. They did not have enough money to build the necessary water line. They had several 5-gallon cans that they filled up with water at Billy's parent's house. And guess who was driving that truck! It was 9-year-old Kenny. He was the family's water boy. This meant that he had to learn to drive the family's pickup truck at the young age of NINE! And even though he was using a pickup, Kenny still had to make several trips a day. After filling the cans, once he was home he still had to haul the cans from the back of the truck to the kitchen. Their stay in the new house lasted from 1954 - 1964. It was then that they moved into a larger home; a home that was fixed just for them at the hands of a few close friends, Ernie Graham, R.J. Crowley, and Lloyd Garrett. The men worked hard fixing up the home for the family. Hours and hours turned into days, that turned into weeks, that turned into months, until finally they happily looked around and said, "We're done." They did not charge the family a single dime. It was work done with love and solid friendship. They especially built the home with the purpose of making things easier for Wanda. In this home, the family now had running water, electricity, and even a washer and dryer. Kenny was also happier to be in a bigger home!

Wanda was also known to be a workaholic. There were days she picked berries until dark. She preserved food and shared extra food with others in need. She had a trailer next to her house where she left preserved and canned food for any who needed it. She hated to see anything go to waste. Once when they were on a trip to Norman they came across a cotton field that had remnants of cotton throughout the field. The cotton picking machine had already made a trip through and left pieces of cotton. She commented that she wished she had a cotton sack to pick up those cotton pieces.

She joined the workforce when the children were young. She worked as a Line Operator at Western Electric. The opening of Western Electric was a major turning point in Oklahoma history. It was the first high tech business to open in the state. Wanda was there to help it grow. The first stage of developing the Western Electric Plant (which is a subsidiary of AT&T) was clouded in mystery. It was so secretive that the officials at the Oklahoma City Chamber of Commerce, who helped find the location for the plant, did not even know who they were talking to until the plans were finalized. The only contact name they had was of a Mr. Cassidy and the only address they had for him was PO Box in New York City. When Mr. Cassidy received the final planned paperwork and location details it took him another five months to agree to open his company there. It was only then that those in Oklahoma found out just who they had been talking to. It all came together May 5, 1957. Western Electric opened a pilot plant that ran for three years until it moved to West Reno street in Oklahoma City. They opened at that location in 1961. It was there that Wanda joined the company.

They made electro-mechanical telephone switching equipment known as cross-bars. Though they struggled to keep up with the demand for their product their goal was to enable every home in the country to have a telephone. It is easy to understand why it was difficult to fill the orders when you remember that employees hand wired each and every device.

Wanda was intelligent and highly skilled at her job. She was soon running her own line and training new employees. It was basically the job of a supervisor. However, the glass ceiling in the work world of the 1960's often blocked women from moving ahead. She may have had the intelligence and capability to do a supervisor's job but she would never be offered the opportunity to carry the title – or earn the salary. Wanda earned 60 cents for every $1 that her male co-worker was paid, doing the same job. Wanda stayed with the company for 31 years. Western Electric would later change their name to AT&T and then to Lucent Technologies in 1996.

After being with the company for 10 years, Bill decided to join Western Electric as well. He was hired to work in the same department as Wanda. She was even the one who trained him. It was not unusual for family members to work alongside each other at Western Electric. Some families had groups of 10-15 family members working there. The company, as a whole, bragged that they were one big family. The company truly looked out for their workers. In the mid-1980's when union workers went on strike, one of the plant managers brought them tents and tables and arranged for the workers on strike to have plenty of refreshments. He felt regardless of the dispute, "providing cold water and a shady place to sit" was the right thing to do on those days since the temperatures were reaching 105 degrees outside.

Unfortunately, standing in one place, along with an assembly line, for 8 hours a day was quite a shock to the system for Billy, a country boy who worked outside his whole life. The factory was hot and crowded. The only sign of the outdoors came from a light shining through a small window on the other side of the room. Bill often fantasized about being back on the farm in the sunshine and breeze. The extreme change soon got to be too much. He was there just short of three months when he decided to approach Wanda about how unhappy he was at the factory. She understood. She knew all too well how countrymen long for the outdoors. His happiness was more valuable than the extra money. The next day, Bill was back on the farm working alongside his dad.

Billy and Wanda went on to have four more children. A son named Jon Edwin was born on Thursday, March 16,

1952. After Jon, they had three daughters. Rhonda Carol Harmon was born on Tuesday, November 24, 1953. Debra Jo Harmon was born on Saturday, February 26, 1955. The baby of the family was Donna Harmon. She was born Tuesday, March 3, 1959. Like most children, Kenny could not pronounce his full name "Kenneth Layne." When Wanda asked him what his name was he would say, "Quify," pronounced Qui-fy. For several years his mom, dad, and Rhonda used "Quify" as his nickname.

Did you know?

Silly Putty is sold in plastic eggs because it was Easter when it was first sold. It cost a dollar when it first came out and it still only costs a dollar. However, it used to be an ounce, now it's only .5 ounce. They stopped selling Silly Putty during the Korean War because there was a restriction on the sale of silicone.

In 1940 the Army held a competition for the design of a vehicle for the military. The Bantham Car Company won the competition with their design of - the JEEP! They were a small company in Butler, Pennsylvania. For some reason, the military did not think that they would be able to fill the order. They gave the design to Ford Motor Company and Wileys Motor Company. It seems that Bantham was never fairly given the opportunity to build their creation but they should always be remembered as the true makers of the JEEP.

When M&Ms were first made, they were sold in tubes and came in 5 colors: red, orange, yellow, green, and violet. Peanut M&Ms came out in 1954 and for the first 6 years, they only came in the color grey. There was no "m" stamped on the candy until 1950.

During the Korean War, 90% of the troops fighting on the side of South Korea, were American troops.

As of April 2018, there are 7,721 American soldiers still unaccounted for from the Korean War. The Defense POW/MIA has a website that updates information on the recovery of soldier remains. The website is: http://www.dpaa.mil/Our-Missing/Recently-Accounted-For/

Cousins, Billy and Glenn Harmon, playing on a makeshift toy.

Billy Harmon was such a happy baby!

Nellie Harmon holding Ronnie Harrison and Nedra Swinney in
1947.

Taking a break from farming for a fishing trip in 1961.

Ann and Joe Humphries at the '61 fishing trip.

More fun on the '61 fishing trip!

Billy Harmon, Lloyd Garrett, Joe Humphries, Ernie Graham, and
R.J. Crowley

Ernie and Kay Graham joined in on the 1961 fishing trip. Ernie was one of the men who helped build the house for Bill and Wanda.

Glen Moore in 2nd grade at Pauls Valley.

Bernice and Claude Swinney in 1956.

High school sweethearts, Billy and Wanda.

Billy Harmon at Humphries Appliances in Blanchard.

The home of Kenneth and Faye Swinney when they lived in Dibble, Oklahoma.

Faye and Kenneth Swinney in Whittier, California, 1949.

A family reunion at Babe and Nellie's home in 1960. It included the Harmons, the Swinneys, the Harrisons and the Merchants! You can see the potato house in the background.

Spending the day at Babe and Nellie's home.

Back to Front: Babe Harmon, Dewey Merchant, Ronnie, Chief, Delta, Sue, Cloma, James, Jerry, Lyda Merchant, A.W., Tommy, Gene Harrison, and Nellie Harmon

Babe Harmon in the military. He is on the far left.

Babe Harmon (2nd from the left) in Montpelier, Ohio, in August 1918.

Blanchard during the 1930's. The Blue Top Tavern was located where the Ray Williams Rodeo Grounds would later be built. Highway 62 would take the place of the Rodeo. Port Lewis is sitting in the foreground, alongside Evert Patton, Clarence Sitton, Johnny White, and Mutt Wilson.

A few of the men that Babe Harmon played baseball with on the sandlot team. Billy Harmon is 2nd from the right.

Curns Harmon at home. A year later he moved in with Babe, Nellie, and Billy.

Babe and Nellie's home in 1969. Faye Swinney and Nellie Harmon are standing on the south porch.

Cleo Swinney, Nellie Swinney, and Chief Harrison spending the afternoon together.

A summer day in the early 1950's. Escaping the hot sun on the porch at Port and Dode Lewis's home. Pictured here are Olga, Joe Bailey, Dean Sharp, John Sharp, Shy Raredon, and Donald Joe Haynes.

Kenny Harmon later became known around the world as Sad Papaw.

Laster Lane – the athlete who Kenneth Layne Harmon
received his middle name for.

Wanda Harmon in 1962.

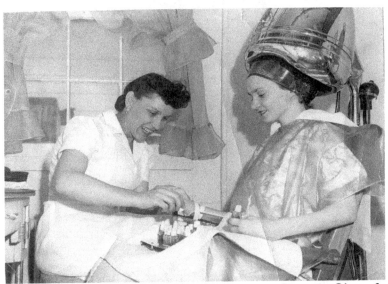

Lillian Harmon, the wife of Curns Jr, ran a Beauty Shop from the front room of her house.

Miss O'Bar was Billy's grade school teacher.

Billy Harmon's 1938 class picture at Dibble School. Billy is in the bottom row, the 3rd from the left. The first boy in that row is his friend, Albert Offolter. Also in the bottom row, the second from the right, is Billy's friend, Kay Sharp. In the 3rd row, the 4th from the left is Buddy McClain. In the top row, the 7th from the left is Charlene Perrin (before the families were related).

Wanda Perrin's class photo in Dibble, 1939. Wanda is in the top row, the 2nd from the left. Roley Richey is in the bottom row, 4th from the left.

The remains of the original Highway 39. This is the dirt road that Billy Harmon used to sneak away to run off to his cousin's house. The road extended from Tabler to Purcell. In 1936, they started work on the new Highway 39. The trees on the left are now at the south side of the road. The road extended between the trees. These remains may be the only part of the original Highway 39, that was not plowed or farmed.

Chapter 3

Harmon Family Farming Years

Following the Land Run on April 22, 1889, farms quickly popped up across the state. By 1907, the President of the State Board of Agriculture wrote "agriculture is, and will be for years to come if not forever, the leading industry in our State." The most appealing part of Oklahoma for farmers was the red dirt. The mixture of sand, siltstone, and shale is what gave the dirt its red color. Farmers were told it was prime for farming, that the red dirt was healthy for crops. It was a promotional idea. However, they were spot on! What they did not realize is that it was also mixed with high volumes of iron which also mixed into their crops. Still does! Brian Carter, Professor of Soil Science at Oklahoma State University, explained that it was during the Permian Geologic Era nearly 300 million years ago that the mixture first came together to give the soil its famous red color.

Oklahoma farmers did not always have it easy. Mother Nature fought against them all year. There was flooding, crushing hail storms, tornadoes, insect infestations and harsh droughts. The worst drought was in 1891. Things were so bad that the railroads (who often drove down the price of their crops), donated bags of seeds to help them grow their crops. The farmers stayed strong. In 1890, the census bureau reported that there were 8,826 farms in Oklahoma. By 1910, the state had 190,192 farms. Among the state's farmers were the Harmons. From the first day the state opened their borders to early settlers, the Harmons made Oklahoma their home.

In 1929, Babe, a farmer since the age of seven, found a new way to sell his crops. He and Cecil started loading up his '29 Chevy to haul produce into Oklahoma City to sell to store merchants. They called them "truck crops." He also sold from a stand that he set up on the side of the road. Cecil enjoyed sharing the farmer's favorite joke of how to tell the difference between Republicans and Democrats shopping for produce. A Republican would stop, ask for the price of the watermelons, then make a face and drive off but the Democrat would smile and say, "I'll take two." At this time, America was entering the Great Depression and most people no longer had the money to buy from them. It was a difficult struggle for the Harmons and their customers.

Babe worried all the time about being able to support his family and keep the farm operational. Stress, being one of the worst things for the human body, soon had Babe in the hospital with ulcers. A year later the ulcers grew worse and he was mostly bedridden. This was greatly uncomfortable for Babe to get used to it. All his life he worked from sun-up til sun-down. And now he was barely able to get out of bed. This can put anyone in a state of depression. He had to find ways to entertain himself. One thing he did was to play with his cat. He tied a button onto a piece of string and would toss it across the room. When the cat reached for it, he would slowly start to slide it back, watching her swat at it along the way. Billy was five years old, at the time, and would stop in every day to see his dad. They had makeshift arm wrestling contests where Babe would hold up his arm and say, "Try to pull my arm down." It entertained Billy to "beat his dad" in the contest every time.

It took over a year, but with the help of Dr. White, Babe recovered enough to be able to go back to work. In 1934, he bought a new car and took out the back seat, making room to haul produce into Oklahoma City. On those days, he always carried a variety of produce, that included one type of cantaloupes and two types of watermelons. In fact, the Harmons would continue to sell the majority of their crops to families and businesses for more than 40 years to come.

By 1950, Babe Harmon grew to witness great strides made in the farming industry. When he was a child, farming alongside his dad, there was a piece of equipment for each step from planting to harvesting. All of the work was done by walking – the plowing, harrowing, and even hand planting the seeds. It took 75-90 hours to produce 100 bushels of corn (approximately 2 ½ acres). By 1890, that time was cut down to 35 – 40 hours. Two years later, in 1892, the gasoline tractor was introduced. This was a great accomplishment to the farming industry. By 1950, with the proper farming equipment (most of which was now automatic) it took 10 – 14 hours of labor to harvest those same 100 bushels of corn.

By this time, Billy had also grown to be a farming man in his own right. Babe found himself not only working alongside his son, but also with his brothers, Cecil, Curns jr, and Jess. When Kenny was 8 years old, he joined the ranks of Harmon men and started working alongside them on the farms. Jess also hired three hired hands, Hunk, Sharky and Hoss Roath Cecil and Hoss were close friends and farming partners for many years. Hunk and Jess also dabbled on the side, making homemade beer. Choctaw Beer, referred to as, "Choc Beer" was a popular homemade beer at that time. Homemade Choc Beer was first made in 1894 with a combination of barley, hops, tobacco, fish berries, and a small amount of alcohol. By 1950, the recipe changed to a mixture of barley, hops, sugar, and yeast (combined with rice and oats), and mashed apples, peaches, or raisins (that part was optional). They were just some of the few bootleggers in Oklahoma at that time.

Meanwhile, back on the farm, the crops were still thriving. The majority of the crops raised on the Harmon farms were cantaloupes and melons, which grew exceptionally well in the grainy soil. They grew several types of watermelons, such as the Tender Sweet (yellow inside), Charleston Gray, Garrisonian watermelon, Cobb Jim, Black Diamond, and Jubilees. In the late 1950's, Billy grew into a farmer himself. In 1959, he had an idea for a new melon and began planting the seeds of Black Diamond and Cobb Jim together. He decided to plant the seeds together and the bees would cross the two together and create his new melon a new type of melon that would carry the best qualities from each one. It worked! His creation was a Diamond-Cobb watermelon. It was the most successful selling melon in all their 80 years of growing watermelons on their farms. In 1966, at the height of its success, one of Diamond-Cobb watermelons weighed in at 102 pounds. It was the largest one ever grown on the family farm. They named the watermelon, "King Cross." in the neighboring community of Rush Springs, they hold a contest every year for the largest watermelon. The Harmon watermelon outweighed their prized melon.

Their watermelons were so popular that 3-5 times a week they took three truckloads of melons into town to sell. Babe took two truckloads on his route through Northeast Oklahoma City. Billy took his truckload into the Farmer's Market on Reno Avenue. The first trips in town were in the first week of July and usually included 100 bushels of cantaloupes or 100 watermelons. The number carried in one trip depended on whether or not the sideboards were up and the size of the watermelons and cantaloupes. There is only so much weight that a pickup truck can handle. But, then again, Kenny recalled a time in 1964 when a man bought 11 of the 90-pound Diamond-Cobb cross watermelons. He fit them all in his car. He was hauling them all the way to California! Kenny, Babe, and Billy truly enjoyed the interaction with their customers.

In 1958, even though Babe owned 330 acres of his own land, he decided to rent more land from Joe Davis, just two miles north of Blanchard. There he grew sweet potatoes and more cantaloupes. Kenny remembers the sweet potato planter being quite unique. There were two seats for one person to sit on each side. Those two took turns dropping plants into the furrow cut out by the planter. There was a place for a bushel basket between the two planters. There were also two sets of discs on the planter – one in front and one in back. The front set of discs cut out the furrow. The discs in the back covered the furrow.

Author Notes: Joe Davis's sons, Sam and John, tried to get 8-year-old Kenny to pee on an electric fence. He already knew the dangers of the fence and refused the dare. His brother, Jon, took them up on it. He never did it again!

In 1958, they started selling less at their stands and more to the stores and restaurants. By 1963, they made up their entire customer list. One of their best stores was Grider's, at South 29th Street and May Avenue (one of Oklahoma City's busiest intersections). Grider's did not buy the watermelons, however, they bought loads of cantaloupes. Vernon, the store manager, did allow the Harmons to pedal the watermelons in their parking lot. Kenny was only 13 years old when he sold watermelons with them. He became a pro at pedaling and making change for customers.

They used working mules on the farm until the mid '50's. Raising hogs and cattle was also a large part of their farm. In the 50's they raised Short Horn Cattle. By the 60's they switched to raising Angus Cattle. For the Short Horn Cattle, they grew Sudan Hay as feed. When they changed over to the Angus Cattle, they grew Hybrid Sudan (Sudex) hay to feed to them instead. The hay was stored inside the barn until it was full. After that it was stacked outside the barn.

Working cattle was a year-round job. In the rain, sun, and snow. It did not matter. They had to be fed daily. As the temperatures warmed up, they started planting hay. From the end of May through June, they started baling and hauling hay. If there was too much rain, then it was put off until July and August. In October, the grass started to dry up. From then until spring, the cows were fed hay in the barn. They were fed by hand in the stalls. Each cow and Yearling was in their own stall. During spring, the cows were also fed cottonseed hulls, cottonseed mill and sometimes ground maize. The hulls and cottonseed mills were hauled from Oklahoma City in the back of Babe's two-ton 1950 Chevy truck, with the three sideboards. The hulls were loaded on the steel bed up to the top of the 3-foot sideboards. A tarp was then thrown on top. From there, 100 pound sacks of mill were placed on top of the tarp. When he arrived back home, Bill and Kenny unloaded the sacks of mill. Eleven-year-old Kenny would then drive the truck up to the feedlots and unload the hulls with a scoop shovel. Kenny remembers it being "mighty good workout for a farm boy."

Babe referred to his hogs as "mortgage lifters," because of their value. When Kenny grew strong enough to carry a filled 5-gallon bucket then it became his job to feed slop to the hogs. Babe had a rowdy sow who would run between Bill's legs, knocking him down, which sent the slop flying. Kenny was extremely happy when Babe sold the hogs and focused solely on the cows. Sadly, during one spring, the calves became infected with the Blackleg disease. They could not single out the source of the disease because it can come from several different forms of bacteria. The disease kills calves within 12 hours of infecting them. During this outbreak, more than a dozen of Babe's calves died. After the outbreak ended the top layer of grass and soil had to be destroyed because the bacteria from the Blackleg disease can live in the soil for many years, reinfecting the calves. This was not the case on the Harmon farms, the soil was not affected. The 7 way clostridial vaccine for Blackleg was discovered in 2005.

They had more than just animals on the farm. At one point, Kenny had 20 pet cats. His favorite was a mama kitty named, Susie. She was the friendliest towards him. When he would stoop to the ground she would climb on his back and shoulders. When the family started to have a problem with mice crawling through the hay, Kenny would stroll into the barn with his cats behind him. As Kenny overturned bales, the mice would scurry, not knowing what hit them.

To Kenny, the hardest work was in the fields with the cantaloupes and watermelons. They used a plow called a Walking Cultivator. This tool had two sweeps on the left and right side of the plow. Each plow had one long wooden handle. The sweeps moved sideways between and around the plants. All of the sideways movement was by the strength of the man behind the Walking Cultivator. When the cantaloupes and watermelons reached a certain width, the Cultivator could no longer be used. Then out came the Hoe to replace the Cultivator.

Kenny always thought the most dreaded sight of all the farm work was the sight of the weeds, that they called "careless weeds." Just after sunrise, they would check on the rows (1/8 mile long) for any growth of the careless weeds. They could grow several inches in a week and come in as thick as the hair on a dog's back. They worked hard to prevent the careless weeds from growing. At full size, the careless weeds resembled something more like a small tree. They could grow over 6 feet tall and 4 inches in diameter. The seed packs that clung to the careless weeds had tiny thorns, shaped like spikes.

From 1962-1967, Babe rented 250 acres of farmland, 5 miles southwest of Blanchard on a lot called The Wilkins Place. The Wilkins land was on the south side of the Giles Ranch. The farm included a hay barn and a spring fed creek. Babe, Bill, and Cecil Harmon had three fields to farm that included several types of crops. The fields were spread apart on the farm. They included seven acres on the west field, ten acres on the east field, and on the north field were another 20 acres. The broomcorn shed, which was used as a hay barn, had an acre field next to it that was more like a large garden spot. The biggest problem was when they had to cross the creek to access the north field. This was especially true when they had to carry loads of melons or cantaloupes to the south field. Some of the Harmon family's most difficult days farming occurred in the North Field. Among the 5 acres of crops there were tomatoes, cucumbers, maize (corn), oats, wheat, okra, squash, and turnips. They also grew sweet sorghum. Out of curiosity, Kenny tasted it just to see if it was sweet. It was! Sudan Hay and Sudex Hay were grown to feed to the cattle. The crops that made the most money for them were always the watermelons and cantaloupes. For the cantaloupes, the stores paid $1 for every 3 or $3 for a basket. There were 15 cantaloupes in every basket. Some of the cantaloupes grew to the size of a small watermelon.

Though farming was in his blood, there were days that Kenny found the work to be grueling. Once early in the morning, Kenny arrived just after sunrise. He looked eastward down the rows of weed-filled melons to check on the progress but it was too difficult to see a single thing. He knew that most of that hot day would be spent with a hoe in hand. The only thing he looked forward to was jumping into the spring-fed swimming hole located on the west end of the field. Taking a dip in the cool water was a great way to relax at the end of a day of hard farming work. He spent countless days feeling the sun beating down on him. As backbreaking as the work can be, Kenny will never forget those years working at the Wilkins Ranch. Some of his best experiences were the days he spent hauling hay with Bill and AB Smith.

Babe was a hardworking farmer but in his heart, he was also a huge baseball fan. He even took a break from farming when Cardinals baseball games were on the radio. He played every home game on the radio and gave his farm hands an extra long lunch break during the games.

Enemies of the farmers were animals that liked to devour their crops. The rabbits ate the cantaloupes and the crows ate the watermelons. And worse than that - the insects. Insects were always a big threat to the melons and cantaloupes. In the 60's the Harmons began using Parathion to control the insects. It was also called Folidol. The pesticide was a brown liquid that smelled like rotting eggs and garlic. The color became a darker brown under the hot sun. It was added to the crops by spraying it on. The sprayer was pulled by a tractor. However, Parathion is dangerous and highly toxic. If any of the Harmon men or their workers would breathe in too much it would have been fatal. The directions were perfectly clear. One of them being: Do not spray if the winds are not calm, this meant even if there was only a slight wind....DO NOT SPRAY. Another rule was that the plants can be moist but not wet or the Parathion would roll off the leaves. And most importantly, after they sprayed the Parathion, they were to stay out of the fields for a minimum of 24 hours. For that reason, spraying was usually done in the morning. Well, one afternoon, Cecil sprayed the west field and the next morning entered the farm thinking enough time had gone by. He never really believed the Parathion was as dangerous as they said. He did not get too far into the field when he realized his mistake. His head started pounding. He became dizzy and everything he saw around him became blurry. He had extreme difficulty breathing. He tried to leave the area but was stumbling and grew confused on which direction to go. He escaped just before being overcome by the poison.

Parathion is also highly combustible chemical which could bring on more problems if a fire broke out because the traditional bunker gear worn by firefighters could not protect their skin from being burned by the toxic chemical. So, if the area or the equipment would catch fire it could only be put out by letting it burn itself out. It would not be until 1992 when it would finally be banned from fruit, nut, and vegetable crops. Though it would continue to be allowed for use on cotton, rice, and fruit trees. There were 23 countries to ban it outright and push to have it banned worldwide. In spite of what it did to the people, and the fact that over 600 farmers were poisoned (that's just the ones that were reported), and another 100 farmers were killed by it, their main concern was what it was doing to the bees, fish, birds, and other wildlife.

Kenny Keeler, a friend of the Harmons, was known as Dibble's best storyteller. To Keeler, some of his favorite stories were about the Harmons activities out on the fields. There was an occasion when Cecil announced that it was time to plant the crops; Hoss disagreed. Well, Cecil ignored him and plated anyway. That afternoon, Kenny drove by and saw Hoss plowing everything that Cecil just planted. Keeler described it as "Cecil was planting and Hoss was plowing behind him." Another one of Keeler's favorite stories about Hoss was from one morning in the spring, he drove by to see Hoss planting melons. That afternoon he drove by again only to see Hoss already spraying the fields. Hoss said he was spraying because he did not want the bugs out there waiting for the lopes to come up. Hoss was known for being impatient but on this day his impatience was becoming destructive because spraying too soon would prevent the melons from growing at all.

Though the farm was mostly successful, there were times when they barely hung on from one year to the next. During those difficult years of farming and financial struggles, Nellie had her own army behind her to give her family a light on the dark days. A silent army – her church family. A group of close-knit friends and prayer warriors whose spiritual beliefs ran so deep that they deserve a chapter all to themselves.

Did you know?

There are Pizza Farms in the Midwest that grow all of the ingredients used to make a pizza. Some of the farms even divide their crops into slices.

If you tap on a watermelon and it makes a hollow sound, that means it is ripe.

There are over 300 varieties of watermelon grown in the United States but only 50 are sold in the stores. By the way, that square watermelon that is sold in Japan is made into a square by putting a glass jar around it as it grows. And it costs $82!

The St. Louis Cardinals were formed in 1882. Their original name was the Brown Stockings. They became the Cardinals in 1900.

In the 1930's, the Cardinals players, Pepper Martin, Joe "Ducky" Medwick, and the Dean brothers, Dizzy and Daffy, were called the Gashouse Gang because they looked like troublemakers from New York's Gashouse district.

A load of watermelons on Cecil Harmon's 1936 Inter-National truck. Blanchard's POD Francis Ford Dealership is in the background.

Their hard farming work is about to pay off. Pictured here is Cecil Harmon, Henry Cole, Clay Richey, and Babe Harmon.

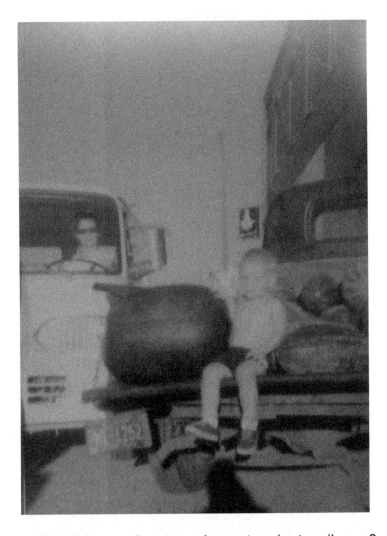

Their giant 102-pound watermelon put a giant smile on 3-year-old, Guy Graham's, face. Guy is the son of Ernie and Kay Graham. The melon outweighed the champion melon at Rush Springs competition that year. Their winning melon came in at 96 pounds.

Babe Harmon was one of the hardest working farmers in Oklahoma history. The hay barn in the background was where Kenny took his cats to catch mice. It is also the barn where he offloaded the '50 model 2 ton Chevy truck, full of cottonseed hulls

Cecil Harmon in 1930 with the Walking Cultivator rigged to a team of mules. That same plow was later rigged to a tractor.

Babe Harmon and Nellie Harmon at home on their family farm.

Father and Son ~ Babe Harmon and Billy, in 1931.

Jess Harmon's hired hand, Sharkey (middle), with Billy and Glenn, in 1931.

Chapter 4

Church Days

The Harmon family foundation has a history of farming and a rich spiritual heritage. A belief that began in the halls of Jellico Creek Church more than 100 years ago now continues at the Blanchard Trinity Free Holiness Church. The church, located at the corner of S. Van Buren Ave and E. Broadway Street, was founded in 1938 by Gene Richey, Tom Richey and Sly Richey, Cecil Lambert, Carl Smalley, Grover Andrews, Ed Wayland, and Ed Norris under the name Blanchard Apostolic Church. In the early 70's, the name was changed to Trinity Free Holiness. Nellie's first key role with the church was to teach Sunday School to the teens. She remained with the church for 30 years.

Nellie was the first of the Harmons to attend the Blanchard church in the early 40's. Nellie was a praying wife and mother and often referred to the church's prayer groups as "Help Meets." Kenny fully believes that it was her prayers that made a big difference for her family.

Kenny's first Bible lessons began at Nellie's house. He was almost 10 years when his grandmother started having Bible Study in her house. Kenny was invited to participate, especially since some of their friends had children of their own. His cousin, Anita Ruth, was also there. Some of Nellie's friends that participated in Bible Study were Buzz and Mable Harmon and Helen Garrison. Lorene Brandon gave Nellie rides to church. Sometimes she visited Nellie for their own Bible Study meeting. Her children Pam and Gayla would play together while Lorene and Nellie enjoyed their fellowship. Nellie cherished her Bible studies so much that she would meet with anyone at any time.

Nellie was one of the Elders in church, along with, Tom and Bertha Richey, Sister Creswell, Sister Minnie Mitchusson, Cecil & Lois Lambert, Brother Lem Moore, who was deaf, and Sister Moore, who was blind. Nellie was referred to as "Sister Nellie." At the church, it was considered disrespectful if you did not call the men "brother" and the women "sister." Nellie was sometimes so happy when entering the church she would dance in the spirit before the start of service. Nellie rode to church with Lorene Brandon from Alex, Oklahoma.

Nellie was a devout Christian who dedicated much of her time to serving the church. She taught Bible class and often volunteered at different church functions. During the 50's and early to mid 60's, Nellie had Bible study in her home. Some of those who attended were Buzz and Mable (and their children Wayne and Anita Ruth Harmon), Sister Lorene Brandon and her children (Pam and Gayla), and Helen Garrison (a neighbor that lived less than a mile from Nellie.

Kenny grew close to several people in the church. His best friends were Jerry Hall, Lowell Williams, Larry Hager, and Richard Ashford. Hall played the steel guitar for the church choir. Brother Dovey George grew to become a mentor to Kenny at church. He reflects fondly that "He was one of the best men I ever knew. He spoke with humility, wisdom, patience, love. Brother Dovey was Pastor of the Holiness Church for more than 25 years. His years of service ran from the 1950's to the 1970's.

Port Lewis and his family also became new friends to the Harmons at church. Both families started attending close to the same time. Port had an amazing experience that brought him to the church. A few weeks prior, he fell ill to the point that he was put on the critical list in the hospital. His family was informed that he may not survive. That night he had a dream of his mother, who had passed away. She was urging him to follow her up a narrow path. Not far off was a second path that was wide and smooth. He approached the path that his mother directed him to and he proceeded to follow her. At the end of the path was a scene that he described as Heaven. He not only survived the night but walked out of the hospital feeling just fine and went home. The visit with his mother rejuvenated his whole spirit and attitude toward life. A euphoria that brought him through the doors of Blanchard Trinity Free Holiness Church. His son, Pruitt Lewis describing the change in him as simply unbelievable. Before the experience, he cursed fluently. After the experience, he never uttered another foul word. He once smoked cigars heavily but threw nearly a full box in the garbage. He never smoked them again – not once. He also gave up alcohol for good. After he started attending church he was saved and spent the rest of his life serving the Lord.

For Kenny, attending the church was made easier by the friendship of Jerry and Lowell. Before they became friends in church, Jerry and Kenny already knew each other from the baseball field. Kenny played for Dibble and Jerry played for Blanchard. Kenny noted that Jerry was an ace baseball player for Blanchard High School. He previously met Lowell through his grandmother. Lowell was Lorene's nephew.

They would hang out before and after church. During one Sunday afternoon, Sonny Price was showing them a car that he just bought. It was a '57 Chevy with a 2-speed transmission called Power Glide. He only had it for a couple of days, when their friend, Jerry Price asked to drive it. They were hopped up with excitement and showing off as they sped off. They got a block down the road when Jerry lost control and put the car on its side.

The men developed lifelong friendships. Kenny and Lowell first became friends mainly because they had a common interest – in girls! They were both girl crazy! As adults, Larry and Richard sought careers as Iron Workers, as Kenny also do. The three men worked side-by-side. One of the greatest benefits of growing up in a small town is having the chance to build these lifelong friendships.

Author Notes: The bedroom community of Alex, Oklahoma was founded by and named for William Vinson Alexander. He began to lay out the plans for the community in 1885. Alexander was also the first to open a business there, a General Store that would also house the town's first post office. His wife, Martha, was appointed as the town's first Postmaster.

The community was almost completely wiped out on July 7,

1906, when a tornado touched down, clearing away almost everything in its path. The people came together, stronger than ever, they gave it their all to rebuild their business district. A year later, they came back with a drug store, a variety store, and three General stores. On October 3rd of that same year, Alexander opened the First State bank. The town also now had their own newspaper, the Alex Tribune. In 1910, they were officially incorporated as a community.

Did you know?

A brand new 1957 Chevrolet Bel Air cost $2,511 when it debuted.

The '57 Chevy Bel Air included a tissue dispenser and an Autotronic Eye that sensed the light from oncoming traffic and dimmed headlights automatically.

In 1631, a publishing company published a Bible with the typo "Thou Shalt Commit Adultery." Nine of those Bibles exist today. They are called the Sinner's Bible.

The Geneva Bible is the first Bible to use numbered verses. It is also the Bible Shakespeare used and the one that the Pilgrims brought to America in 1620.

The last word in the Bible is Amen.

Kenny spending time with his family before church, in 1968.

Babe and Nellie with Dewey and Lyda Merchant. Nellie and Lyda were sisters.

Chapter 5

A Sweeter Side of Kenny's World

Charlie Lee Perrin and Icie Josephine Hill

As close as the members of the Harmon family grew to be, there was another half of Kenny's world, a softer side – the Perrins. This was Wanda Harmon's side of the family, Kenny's mother. Her parents were Charlie and Icie Perrin. Charlie Perrin's family came to America from England. He met Icie in the early-1900's. After they were married, their first home was a tent in Dibble. This situation came upon them after they were conned by an attorney. Charlie and Icie were in the last role for people to sign up and claim Oklahoma property. The attorney they hired (with the last of their money), was supposed to file the paperwork showing Icie's Native American heritage. However, he ran off with their money, leaving them penniless and homeless. The couple stayed strong and credit their faith with helping them through that. Icie was deeply religious and often went to the creek to pray. Their first child, Floetta, was born inside the tent. She was two years old when the family moved from the tent to their first home in Chickasha, a neighboring community to Dibble. They had eight children together, Floetta Inez (Moore), Jack Charles, Armon, Charlene, Mary Sue (Hollis), Gaylon, Wanda (Harmon), and Mona (Derryberry).

The Perrins were pretty special to Kenny in his youth. They all treated him with love and kindness. Collectively they were the best family that he ever knew. It was at their home in Chickasha that Kenny and his family visited them the most. He remembers his Paw-Paw Perrin (Charlie) as a sweet, kind, elderly man. It was hard on Kenny when his grandparents separated. The break-up was rocky and caused rifts in the family. Icie did not drive and after Charlie left her, she relied on her children to take her where she needed to go. Though Kenny continued to respect his grandfather, (because that is how he was raised), he was never able to forgive him for leaving his grandmother and their eight children, who were all still at home. Charlie, on the other hand, later regretted his decision to make that move.

Mona was the first of their children to move away. She and her husband, Kenneth Derryberry, moved to California with their twin daughters, Linda and Brenda. She made the move in the mid 50's.

Their daughter, Charlene, moved to Enid, Oklahoma with her husband, Larry Stamper, and their son, Johnny Allen. Even though it was only 2 ½ hours away, it was still too far for the family to travel to. Every summer the family had huge get-togethers that Kenny always enjoyed, especially because it meant hanging out with his favorite cousin, Glen. Unfortunately, Charlene could not attend these either.

Kenny was 11 years old when his Aunt Sue married Logan Able and she moved to Opelousas, Louisiana. Opelousas is a large city so it was new and exciting for them. Sadly though, it was an 8-hour drive from Dibble so visits would come down to a few weeks in the summer and usually a week at Christmas time. From there they moved to Wynnewood, Oklahoma, where he worked at the Kerr McGee Refinery. In Wynnewood, they only lived seven miles south of Pauls Valley.

Jack moved to Pauls Valley in the mid 1950's to work for his brother-in-law, George Moore, at George's Radiator Works. He later suffered from his exposure to Agent Orange. This cost him his life and he died of Leukemia in the 70's. He was the first of Charlie and Icie's children to pass away.

Armon Perrin worked for JC Penney when it was inside the Chickasha Mall. The store closed in March 2000. Armon moved to Texas to stay with the company. Gaylon, the youngest of the Perrins, also moved to Texas, years earlier, to start a successful auto body repair business. He helped Armon get settled in when he made the move to the Lone Star State.

Out of all of Kenny's aunts and uncles, he spent the most time with George and Floetta. Mostly because Wanda and

Floetta were always so close growing up. Kenny was the same age as their son, Glen.

Wanda doted on all of the babies and they loved her back just as much. She had a loud voice but it was still soft as a baby's. Gayla, Sue's daughter, swears she remembers Wanda looking down at her when she was in her crib. Gayla holds a treasure of memories inside that include the smallest sights and sounds. These include the heavy cast iron stove that Billy and Wanda had tucked in the corner of the kitchen inside their potato house and the feeling of the old down mattresses that were stuffed full of feathers.

Sue came in every summer to visit the family. Kenny's sister, Donna was close in age to her daughter, Gayla. The girls grew to be just as close as their mothers. They even called each other "sister-cousins." It seemed to be Gayla and Donna's favorite times of the year. They spent two-three weeks with them every summer and came in again for two weeks at Christmas time.

It was always difficult for the girls to say good-bye. They used to try to create ways to trick their mothers into letting Gayla stay with them when it was time to leave. Once they hid Gayla in the closet, sending the parents on a search. They thought that just maybe, the parents would give up looking and just go home without her.

Nellie and Babe took Gayla under their wings, as though she were one of their own granddaughters. Gayla remembers fondly that Nellie had long hair and she used to let Donna brush it. Gayla was jealous because she wanted to brush her hair too. Donna would tell her that she was not done yet and she can have a turn when she is finished. Gayla never did get a turn.

They used to sneak into the watermelon field and crack open a watermelon to eat for an afternoon snack. That same evening they could hear Babe grumbling, "Someone's been in that watermelon field again." They later realized that he knew it was them and he just said that to tease them. When they were teens Billy decided since they want to play alongside the crops then they were going to put them to work. He paid them to pick tomatoes. By the end of the day, their arms and legs were green in color and itchy all over. They jumped in the creek behind the tomato patch to wash off and soothe the itchiness. One afternoon a huge bright neon-green snake decided to slither in and join them. This sent the girls screaming back home!

Did you know?

There are over 1,200 varieties of watermelon grown around the world.

In Israel and Egypt, watermelon is served with feta cheese.

The hairbrush, as we know it today, was breated in 198, by Lyda A. Newman.

Sam Walton's first job was at J.C. Penney. He was a Management Trainee and was paid $75 a month. Walton later became the founder of Walmart.

Andrew Jackson was President when the plan for the Trail of Tears was made. However, Martin Van Buren was President when the plans were actually executed. Today, only Andrew Jackson is blamed for the horrific event.

John and Kenny Harmon at their Granny Perrin's house in 1956

Jack and Joyce Perrin with their firstborn son, Jackie Don.

The Perrin sisters: Wanda, Floetta, Charlene, Sue, Ramona (Mona)

Icie Perrin and Mona Perrin with the twins, Linda and Brenda DerryBerry.

Gary Moore, the oldest child of George and Floetta, was trained to work on nuclear subs in the Navy.

Gaylon Perrin also served proudly.

Charlene Beaver, Anthony Beaver, Billy Harmon and Gaylon
Perrin at Icie Perrin's home in Chickasha.

George Moore and Armon Perrin enjoying snacks!

Billy Harmon, Armon Perrin, and Gaylon Perrin (background)
at Billy and Wanda's home in 1955.

Mona with the twins, Linda and Brenda DerryBerry.

Wanda with Jackie Don Perrin and Gary Moore on her lap.

Floetta, Charlie, and Icie Perrin on happier days.

Young Love ~ George and Floetta Moore

Doug Perrin hoisted on top of Kenny's '65 SS 396 Impala

George Moore, Kenny Harmon, Bill Harmon, and Glenn Moore at George and Floetta's home in Pauls Valley on 116 S. High Street.

Billy Harmon, Sue Perrin, and Johnny Allen Stamper (Charlene's oldest son) at 1609 Colorado Avenue in Chickasha.

Armon and Barbara Perrin with Doug and Diane Perrin.

Celebrating Easter at Billy and Wanda's house in 1955. Icie Perrin is holding Debbie Harmon. Rhonda is in front holding her Easter basket.

Chapter 6

Oklahoma Lawmen

In 1870, before Oklahoma became a state, the area was known as Indian Territory or the "Five Civilized Tribes." They consisted of the Cherokee, Chickasaw, Choctaw, Creek, and Seminole Indians. The Tribes had their own government, police, and courts. However, they did not have the authority to arrest anyone who was not Indian. That was the job of the US Marshals. And the Marshals could only arrest an Indian if they committed an offense against a man that was any race other than Native American. Among the early settlers of the Indian Territory was a slew of criminals. At the time, crime was running rampant and the tumultuous criminal activities included murder, rape, robbery, bootleggers, cattle thieves and train holdups.

In 1875, Ulysses S. Grant took steps to reign in the trouble that was boiling over in the Indian Territory. Grant appointed Judge Isaac Parker to establish work with the US Marshals and create a tight system of justice to put an end to the disarray. Some of the marshals who went to work for Parker were Bass Reeves, Bud Ledbetter. Bill Tilghman, Chris Madsen, and Heck Thompson. Bass Reeves is the only Law Enforcement Officer in Oklahoma history that served from the time the area was Indian Territory to the day they earned their statehood.

After the Oklahoma Land Rush in 1889, signs of new life were popping up all around. Farmers were digging up soil to grow their first crops. The banging of hammers echoed across the countryside as new homes were built. Wagons from out of town carried in merchandise for businesses to open their doors for the first time. With a gleam in their eyes and the American dream in their hearts, they were home. It all became official on November 17, 1907. Oklahoma was now America's 47th state

The Marshals stood as the fine line between criminals and Oklahoma's newest residents. There were no bulletproof vests, K9 partners, or high-speed police cars. Marshals were simple men on horseback, with a brave spirit, a quick draw, and a heart for their community. Holding a compassion to protect the people of Oklahoma is what led them into situations where they were face-to-face with some of history's most dangerous criminals. They had to be every bit as fearless as the men they fought. Historians David Baird and Danny Goble noted that the core values of Oklahoma's first families were optimism, innovation, perseverance, entrepreneurialism, common sense, collective courage, and simple decency. Protecting those values and the families rights to grow in the new state were...and continue to be...the Oklahoma lawmen.

Kenny Harmon grew up with farmers all around him but that was his father's side of the family. Though his mother's side also had farmers, included among them were several members of law enforcement. Claude B. Swinney, who Kenny is a direct decedent of, served as a Garvin County Sheriff. He is known for his capture of Elmer Lee Haggard for the killing of John Hardy Baugh. His Grandfather, Charlie Perrin, was a Police Officer for the Hydro Police Department. Charlie's brother, Hack Perrin, (Kenny's great-uncle), was elected as the Grady County Sheriff. He held that position through the 40's, 50's, and early 60's.

Bass Reeves

Deputy US Marshal

The Oklahoma City Police Department is the oldest police department in Oklahoma. But going back before the days of the OCPD, there were US Marshals that watched over what was Indian Territory. Bass Reeves was among those men. Reeves was born in 1838. Both of his parents were slaves. During the Civil War, he escaped to Oklahoma's Indian Territory and lived with the Cherokee, Seminole, and Creek tribes. The Native Americans took great care of Reeves. They gave him a home, protected him from the law, taught him their language and sharpened his shooting and hunting skills. In fact, his shooting was so sharp and accurate he was barred from their local turkey shoot competitions. Reeves also served with the Union Indian Home Guard Regiments during the Civil War.

In 1865, as the war came to an end, Abraham Lincoln issued the Emancipation Proclamation. Since he was no longer considered a fugitive, Reeves moved on to Van Buren, Arkansas. There he married Nellie Jennie. The couple had 10 children – 5 boys and 5 girls. To support his family he worked as a farmer and also for the Deputy US Marshals. Ten years after reaching Arkansas, Reeves was appointed a Deputy US Marshal by Marshal James Fagan. This made history across the country, for Reeves was now the first African American to be appointed a Deputy Marshal.

By 1907, as Oklahoma was earning their statehood, Reeves was also being recognized for being one of the most successful law enforcement officers in American history for capturing more than 3,000 criminals. One of the arrests was for his own son, who was wanted for the murder of his wife. Being ambidextrous often worked in his favor. He was actually born left-handed, which was considered unlucky, even a hindrance, so he was trained to use his right hand. He carried three pistols with him at all times.

From there he moved onto Oklahoma's Muskogee Police Department. The department was in its ninth year of operation having been established since the town was Indian Territory. Reeves served alongside Bud Ledbetter, who stated that Reeves "never quailed in facing any man." In all of his years in law enforcement and in all of the gun battles that he found himself in, he was never shot by anyone – not once.

Sadly, his career came to an end two years later when he was diagnosed with Bright's disease, a chronic inflammation of the kidneys. The disease causes internal bleeding, hemorrhaging, convulsions, and even blindness and coma. His doctor treated it with warm baths, mercury, opium, diuretics, and laxatives. He also used the medicinal plants, squills, and digitalis, as well as a diet that restricted cheese, red meat, and alcohol.

As his health was failing fast, a local newspaper, the Muskogee Times Democrat, wrote "in the early days when the Indian country was overridden with outlaws, Reeves would herd into Fort Smith, often single-handed, bands of men charged with crimes from bootlegging to murder. He was paid fees in those days that sometimes amounted to thousands of dollars for a single trip, trips that sometimes lasted for months."

Bass Reeves lost his fight to Bright's Disease on January 11, 1910. The next day, the Muskogee Phoenix acknowledged the passing of the legendary lawman stating, "In the history of the early days of Eastern Oklahoma the name of Bass Reeves has a place in the front rank among those who cleaned out the old Indian Territory of outlaws and desperadoes. No story of the conflict of government's officers with those outlaws, which ended only a few years ago with the rapid filling up of the territory with people, can be complete without mention of the Negro who died yesterday. During that time he was sent to arrest some of the most desperate characters that ever infested Indian Territory and endangered life and peace within its borders. And he got his man as often as any of the deputies."

Bill Tilghman, Chris Madsen, and Heck Thompson

The Three Guardsmen

As criminals were turning Oklahoma into a lawless land, the people found themselves needing a hero among the chaos. That was exactly what they got with legendary lawmen Bill Tilghman, Chris Madsen, and Heck Thompson. They were known as the Three Guardsmen. They were famous for their relentless pursuit of criminals. Though Tilghman had sharp accuracy in a gunfight, he was strongly against this type of violence and only used it as a last resort.

William "Bill" Matthew Tilghman was a career lawman during the rough days of the Wild West. He first served as a city marshal in Dodge City, Kansas. He moved to Oklahoma during the land rush in 1889. Shortly after, he was appointed as a Deputy US Marshal in the Oklahoma Territory. It was there that he teamed with fellow US Marshals Henry "Heck" Andrew Thomas and Chris Madsen. The three men worked together so well, they could predict each other's moves and finish the other one's thoughts.

The Wild Bunch Gang, was a nasty group of outlaws that terrorized the communities they rode through; by starting fights that sometimes ended in murder, robbing banks and stores, and holding up trains. The saying goes, "you live by the sword, you die by the sword," as the Wild Bunch would learn, seeing as how each member of the gang died a violent death at the hands of law enforcement. When they first organized they went by the name the Doolin-Dalton Gang. It consisted of Grat Dalton, Bob Dalton, Bill Doolin, George "Bittercreek" Newcomb (also nicknamed Slaughter Kid), Charley Pierce, Dick Broadwell, Emmett Dalton, and Bill Power. During a train robbery in Adair, Oklahoma on July 15, 1892, things went wrong. Throughout the chaos, two guards and two doctors, who were aboard the train, were shot and wounded. One of the doctors died the next day. An argument broke out among them over who was at fault for the botched robbery. Bob Dalton told Doolin, Newcomb, and Pierce that the gang no longer needed them and they parted ways. The three men returned to their hideout in Ingalls, Oklahoma Territory. A few months later, on October 5th, the remaining members of the Dalton Gang were embroiled in a shootout with law enforcement. Emmett Dalton was the only one who survived, despite being shot 23 times.

Doolin quickly regrouped his gang with new members, William "Tulsa Jack" Blake, Dan "Dynamite Dick" Clifton, Roy Daugherty (also called Arkansas Tom Jones), Bill Dalton, William "Little Bill" Raidler, George "Red Buck" Waightman, Richard "Little Dick" West, and Oliver "Ol" Yantis. This was when they adopted the name, "The Wild Bunch." They had a few other names they went by, such as, the Oklahombres, and the Oklahoma Long Riders (this nickname came from the long dusters that they wore).

There were two teenage girls, nicknamed Little Britches and Cattle Annie that followed the gang everywhere they went. They used the girls as look-outs and to keep them informed on the location of law enforcement officers. Often when the law was zeroing in on the gang, the girls helped them escape. Though the gang could wreak havoc, somehow Bill Doolin was well-liked in the community and earned a "Robin Hood" reputation. Because of this, they too would sometimes protect him from law enforcement. On November 1, 1892, this new gang robbed the Ford County Bank in Spearville, Kansas. Over the 16 months that followed, the gang held up the Santa Fe train in Cimarron, Kansas, making away with $1,000 in silver. They had a shootout with US Marshal E.D. Nix and 14 officers, resulting in the death of three deputies and two citizens. After a few months in hiding, the gang robbed a store and a post office in Clarkson, Oklahoma Territory, and the Farmers Citizens Bank in Woodward, Oklahoma Territory. They seemed to be unstoppable.

On March 20, 1894, Nix sent a decree to the Three Guardsmen requesting the capture of the Wild Bunch. The decree stated, "I have selected you to do this work, placing explicit confidence in your abilities to cope with those desperadoes and bring them in—alive if possible—dead if necessary." With help of Bounty Hunters, the Dunn Brothers (Bee, Calvin, Dal, George, and Bill), the Three Guardsmen were able to topple the gang and bring their tyranny to an end. First, Bill Tilghman caught Bill Doolin on January 15, 1896. Deputy Marshal Chris Madsen made the final two captures. The first came on November 7, 1897, when he located Dynamite Dick Clifton and killed him in a shootout. On April 8, 1898, he had the final shootout with Little Dick West. The reign of terror by the Wild Bunch was over.

James Franklin Ledbetter

Deputy US Marshal ~ Muskogee County Sheriff

James Franklin "Bud" Ledbetter, sometimes called "the fourth guardsman," began a career in law enforcement as a guard on board the American Railway Express on the

Missouri Kansas Texas Railroad. It was nicknamed "Katy." In November 1894, Ledbetter's career was about to make a shift. The infamous Cook Gang attempted to rob the Katy only to be stopped in their tracks by Ledbetter. He was the only guard aboard when he came to face-to-face with the Cook Gang, led by Cherokee Bill Goldsby and Jim and Bill Cook. Armed with a Colt Revolver and a Winchester Rifle, he was able to thwart the robbery and send the gang running. This did not come as a surprise to those who knew him, as it was said that "he could shoot the earlobe off of a man and never put a mark on his jaw."

A year later he moved on to Oklahoma Indian Territory to work as a Federal Marshal for Judge Isaac Parker. At the beginning of December 1897, he was called on to capture the Al Jennings Gang. In October, the gang robbed a passenger train near Chickasha and in November they held up a Santa Fe passenger train near Edmond. In early December, Ledbetter and his posse tracked down the gang, injuring a few of the men in a shootout. On December 6, as his posse closed in on the Al Jennings gang, the thieves surrendered peacefully. Near the end of his career, Ledbetter was elected sheriff of Muskogee County. He earned a solid reputation for being an honest and fair man.

Evett Dumas "E.D." Nix

US Deputy Marshal

You can say that the desire to serve was in the blood for Evett Dumas "E.D." Nix. His father was a Deputy Sheriff. His uncle was a County Sheriff. Nix served alongside Tilghman, Madsen, and Thompson to bring down the outlaws of the Wild West. As Deputy Marshal, he orchestrated the demise of the Doolin-Dalton gang. This went down on September 1, 1893, when he led a posse of 27 Marshals into Ingalls, Oklahoma. He heard the gang was hiding out there. Ingalls was a small town that often served as a safe space for fugitives to hide from the law. The residents agreed to do this because the men spent a great deal of money on their businesses and never caused trouble for the townspeople.

On this day, the marshals, led by Nix, approached George Ransom's Saloon. One of the gang members, "Arkansas Tom" Jones, was upstairs in the Ingalls Hotel. He peered out of his window and saw US Deputy Marshal Thomas Houston taking aim and firing at George "Bitter Creek" Newcomb as he was leaving the saloon. Newcomb was shot in the leg. Before he could fire another round, Arkansas Tom, shot Houston, who died the next day. Within seconds an all-out gun battle spilled into the streets of Ingalls. When the smoke cleared and the last bullet was fired, three marshals and two residents were dead, with many more wounded. Arkansas Tom was captured. The rest of the gang escaped, even though every one of them carried a gunshot wound.

At that time there were 150 people that lived in Ingalls. It is now a ghost town located near Stillwater, Oklahoma. It consists of a few deserted buildings and a memorial to commemorate the shootout.

Sadly, Nix's career in law enforcement was short lived. On January 24, 1896, he was dismissed from all duties, after an audit alleged that he misused funds. It wouldn't be until years later that it was discovered that the fee system was chock full of errors and that Nix actually never abused one cent of the funds he was in charge of. After law enforcement, Nix entered the world of business. In 1929, he co-authored the book, "Oklahombres: Particularly the Wilder Ones." The book details the rise and fall of the Doolin-Dalton gang.

Frank Canton

US Marshal/Oklahoma National Guard

Frank Canton was born Josiah Horner on September 15, 1849. When he was 20 years old, he was a cowboy working on a ranch in Henry County, Indiana. Two years later, in 1871, he moved to Texas and started robbing banks and stealing cattle. On October 10, 1874, he got into a gunfight with Buffalo Soldiers, of the 10th Cavalry Regiment. He killed one and wounded another. In 1877, he was arrested for robbing a bank in Comanche, Texas. On route to jail, he escaped from the Texas Rangers and rode straight to Ogallala, Nebraska. He then swore to change his lifestyle.

From there he moved onto Johnson County, Wyoming, and went to work as a Stock Detective for the Wyoming Stock Growers Association. Their primary role was to capture and stop cattle thieves. He was elected Sheriff of Johnson County in 1885. He served the community for seven years. Working with cattle thieves started to make him a bundle of nerves. He had nightmares and he swore he could see the spirits of cattle thieves that were hanged. Thieves, such as, James Averill and Ella "Cattle Kate" Watson, whose hangings were initiated by Canton. To get a new start in law enforcement that did not revolve around cattle thieves, he moved on to Oklahoma. There he was appointed US Deputy Marshal by Judge Isaac Parker.

His most famous arrest came in 1895. He joined a posse to track down Bill and John Shelley, who just escaped from the Pawnee Jail. The men barricaded themselves in a cabin. The standoff lasted five hours. After 800 shots were fired, Canton sent a burning wagon filled with hay into the cabin. The ensuing fire led the men to flee into the hands of Canton and fellow Marshals as they surrendered.

In 1897, Canton grew bored with Oklahoma and traveled to Dawson, Alaska to work as a US Marshal there. The town was at the height of a gold rush. Canton was called in to regain law & order. The town went from a population of 500 in 1896 to a population of 30,000 in 1898. Canton was not used to the bitter cold and numbing temperatures. One of the most dangerous aspects of life in Alaska is extreme exposure to UV rays, brought on by the high altitudes. This was something else that Canton did not know to expect. In 1898, he became snowbound and barely survived the harsh winter. He also suffered from becoming snow blind. This is brought on to overexposure of the sun's UV rays. It is kind of like having sunburn on the eyes. He had to stay indoors for several weeks while his eyes healed and he regained his sight. He continued to brave the elements of Alaska and curbed crime in the entire town of Dawson.

He returned to Oklahoma in 1907 and was appointed Adjutant General for the Oklahoma National Guard. Though he was proud of his work in law enforcement, he still ached from living a lie – that lie is that his true identity was Josiah Horner and he was a wanted fugitive in Texas. He arranged a meeting with Texas Governor Thomas Mitchell Campbell. He spilled the truth about everything – that he was secretly Josiah Horner and all of his past crimes. He was ready to accept any punishment the Governor felt was appropriate. Campbell considered his work in law enforcement and decided to grant him a pardon. He chose to continue using the name "Canton."

Stringer Fenton

Chief of Police

Stringer Fenton was a small quiet man with a keen eye, a quick wit, and an alert body with muscles of steel. When he first moved to Oklahoma, His goal was to be a farmer. He was quickly attracted to law enforcement, who was equally impressed with his courage and strength. His first position in law enforcement was that of Chief of Police in Cleveland, Oklahoma. In 1903, he also served as a Deputy US Marshal in Osage Oklahoma, then known as Osage Reservation.

As a lawman, Fenton captured notorious bank and train robbers Martins and Simons. In his pursuit to capture another bank robber, Henry Starr, he traced his steps all the way to Phoenix, Arizona. He moved swiftly in this arrest, he caught him on May 5, 1910, took him from Arizona to Colorado and had him back in Oklahoma by the 25th. Still another impressive capture was that of a heinous desperado named C. Henry. He murdered two people and was suspected of killing five more. He was able to elude police for two years until Fenton joined the search. His days of running were over. Fenton had a disdain for bootleggers and single-handedly confiscated nearly 100 carloads of whiskey.

Fenton shot a number of outlaws through the years but

swore that each time was in self-defense. Though it was suggested that he can bring them in "dead or alive," he preferred to bring criminals in alive. He was shot by outlaws on three different occasions. His worst injuries came on December 26, 1914. Al Crain was robbing a pool hall and held 25 men hostage inside while he robbed them of cash and valuables. When Fenton got word of the robbery in progress, he rode in to help. On arrival, Crain turned his gun on Fenton and shot him in the leg. Three more bullets grazed him. Fenton fired back and Crain was killed in the battle. Throughout his career, he won over 100 battles against outlaws and became known to many as one of the best detectives in the country.

Bud Ballew

Deputy Sheriff

When David Monticello Ballew was a young boy in Fannin County, Texas, he was nicknamed "Bud" by his family. At the age of twelve, his father gave him extensive training with guns and taught him to be an excellent horseman. At the tender age of 13, his father sent him out on his own, to live in Ardmore, Oklahoma which was Indian territory at the time. That itself could prove to be dangerous since Native Americans were at war with Europeans. Ballew, however, was able to make peace with the Native Americans in that area.

Three years later his parents and several other family members joined him in Oklahoma. While in Oklahoma he met and fell in love with Fannie Mariah Harper. They later married and had two sons together. He continued to run his ranch, where he chiefly raised cattle for himself and others. The ranch was growing so smoothly that he found himself with extra time and an urge to do more. At this time, the oilfield industry in Oklahoma was beginning to boom. Along with the oil rigs, came a great number of rough characters that worked in the ranks of the oil fields. Ballew dabbled in the oil business but it was still not what he was looking for.

So, when Carter County Sheriff, Buck Garrett, who was also referred to as the Chief Lieutenant, offered him the position of Deputy Sheriff, he did not have to think long to accept and he quickly grew comfortable with his new role.

Without realizing it, this would be one of the best decisions Garrett would ever make. Because it would not be long until Ballew would save his life. Garrett was in pursuit of two men, Charlie Thomas and Arthur "Dusty" Miller, who robbed a man named Jim Taliafero. They were heading towards Ardmore when Garrett was able to catch up to them. A fight broke out between Thomas and Garrett. Miller walked circles around the men trying to get a clear shot at Garrett. This was when Ballew arrived. Miller spun around to turn his aim on Ballew but he was not quick enough. Ballew was able to fire the fatal shot first.

As a Deputy Sheriff, Ballew could often be found in saloons, among the gamblers. The trademark features of 37-year-old Ballew included his stocky build, deep hardy laugh, and the few thick red curls in his hair. He wore a wide-brimmed, dust-colored, cowboy hat and high topped cowboy boots. He was known to be fond of diamonds and often wore a large diamond tie tack. He was also known to be a quick thinker and a fearless man, who could remain calm in the tensest situations. Though known for carrying two guns at all times, he seemed to favor the .45 revolver. Fellow officers noted his attitude as a lawman, stating,"Bud Ballew killed no man except in a clear case of him or me. The killing was done while seeking the arrest of the party." Sadly, during his 12 years of service as a Deputy Sheriff in Ardmore, Oklahoma, he did kill eight men. His first deadly altercation came on November 19, 1915, he walked into a saloon that was being robbed by Pete Bynum, nicknamed Boss Badman of Wirt." During the shootout, Ballew was shot in the stomach. When he returned fire, he killed Bynum. Unfortunately, one of the bullets struck a man named Alison who was fast asleep on a cot in an adjacent room.

Shortly after he recovered from his bullet wound, he was back to work, pursuing and capturing, an outlaw named Steve Talkington. Though Ballew made his best efforts to bring in captured criminals alive, Talkington resisted arrest and Ballew was forced to shoot and kill him. There was a reward for Talkington's capture (dead or alive) and Ballew traveled to Wirt, Oklahoma to meet with City Marshal Highnote and collect payment. When he arrived he found Highnote in a rage. He was fired that morning but he refused to relinquish the position or even leave the building. He also refused to hand over the money to Ballew. A fight ensued and Talkington was shot and killed by Ballew.

The next shooting occurred when he and fellow officer, James Perle, were on a train escorting a prisoner when he jumped from the train to escape their clutches. The officers also jumped to chase after him. They both shot at the prisoner who died at the scene. It is not certain which officer killed the prisoner, it was assumed to be Ballew. A few months later, it was a scuffle with Arch Cambell, in a Barber Shop, that ended with Ballew shooting and killing him.

There was one exception to doing everything possible not to kill anyone. And that was the day he came head-to-head against former U.S. Deputy Marshal Dow Braziel. At the time, Braziel also worked as a Special Officer for the Revenue Service. There was a long-standing feud between the men (that included Garrett), that stemmed over prohibition regulations. Braziel accused both Garrett and Ballew of not enforcing the prohibition laws as aggressively as they should. Braziel was strict with these laws and fought hard to locate and jail moonshiners. His animosity for moonshiners deepened when his peer "Special Officer" Oscar Alexander was killed while attempting to arrest bootleggers the Love brothers. They were returning to Hoxbar, Oklahoma, carrying a case of whiskey from Texas. According to the Love's, they were ambushed by Braziel, Alexander, and their men who were in hiding when they approached. They claimed it was self-defense. Braziel had another version of the events. He stated they shouted for them to STOP and identified themselves as officers, claiming they were fully aware of who they were firing upon.

Garrett and Ballew's cavalier approach to capturing these criminals angered him. Things boiled over for Braziel on Friday, January 31, 1919. Early in the morning, Garrett and Ballew went out for breakfast at the California Cafe, in Ardmore, Oklahoma, at the corner of Main and Mill Streets. Braziel had been there for some time and was seated across the room. Without saying a word....without any warning, he started shooting at Ballew and Garett. Ballew returned fire, shooting Braziel six times. Three bullets struck his left arm, one pierced his skull, one struck his heel, and the fatal shot went through his liver and kidney. Braziel died at the scene. Ballew was arrested and taken to the County Jail. Witnesses spoke on his defense and he was released later that day.

It was his involvement with the Clara Smith case that would put Ballew in the history books. The events of the case unfolded on Sunday, November 21, 1920. Ardmore Oil Tycoon, Jake Hamon, limped into the Hardy Sanitarium with a gunshot wound. He first stated that he was cleaning his gun and it accidentally fired. Hamon died six days later. Though Hamon was a lesser known politician from the small town north of the Red River, his death made national headlines because he was also a Republican National committeeman who was being appointed to a position in President Warren Harding's cabinet.

It was suspected by many in the community that it was his lover, Clara Smith, who pulled the trigger that delivered Hamon's fatal shot. Hamon was married and Smith was his mistress. Several rumors swirled as to what actually happened to Hamon. Some believed that Hamon was abusive towards Smith and that she shot him in self-defense. Still, others believed that Smith shot Hamon for trying to break-up with her. Then were those who even twisted that theory and claimed that Hamon was worried that Smith was going to reveal the details of their affair and he shot himself to avoid a scandal.

Smith left town the day after the shooting which made her look even more guilty. The press hounded Garrett because they believed he knew Smith's whereabouts. Chicago news reporter, Sam Blair, learned that she was in Mexico and he headed there to see. His lead was correct. When he arrived she informed him that she already planned to turn herself into Garrett, who picked her up later that day to escort her back to Ardmore. Upon arrival, her bail was set at $12,000. A group of prominent businessmen paid her bail so that she could be released while she awaited trial. They fully believed that she had to have been justified in shooting Hamon.

The case was brought before District Judge Tom Champion. The prosecutors included Attorney General Prince Freeling, H.H. Brown, and Russell Brown. However, Clara had a heavyweight team made up of attorneys that came in from Chicago and Fort Worth, as well as crackerjack attorneys Jimmy Mathers, Charlie Coakley, and Joe Ben Champion (twin brother of the judge). The trial lasted for seven days, coming to an end on March 17th. From there the jury deliberated for a mere 39 minutes before marching back into the courtroom to declare Clara Smith not guilty.

Reporters covering the trial were mesmerized by the appearance of Ballew and Garrett. The popular quote was that "they look like they stepped off the silver screen playing a wild west movie." They whispered how they did not seem fit in with the modern days of the roaring 20's. The reporters jokingly described them as "two remaining specimens of the wild west sheriffs of the movie reels and yellow backed novels."

Shortly after his retirement from law enforcement, Ballew traveled to Wichita Falls, Texas, to attend a rodeo with his 18-year-old son. They were planning to enter the riding contest. While there, Ballew stopped in at the Denver Domino Parlor, to visit his friends. They owned the parlor. On Friday, May 5th, at approximately 1:35, Ballew was sitting at the counter when Police Chief J.W. McCormick entered with several officers. They claimed they were responding to a disturbance call and when they arrived they found Ballew "joshing with the boys." McCormick approached him from one side, another officer to the opposite side and a detective from behind. McCormick stated that he informed Ballew that he was under arrest. Ballew responded by saying, "You are out of luck," and reached under his coat. At that time, they fired 5 bullets into him. He was immediately taken to a funeral home to be embalmed. Texas doctors contacted Hardy Sanitarium to inform them that Ballew was dead. They flew directly to Texas to pick up his remains. In Oklahoma when his body was examined they did not match the story given by McCormick. It suspiciously looked like all bullets came by behind, or from an angle (but still out of Ballew's sight). Questions would rise over who fired the first bullet and from what direction. These and other questions would never be answered since he was shot at 1:35 and embalmed by 3:15 that same day. Why the rush? What were they trying to hide? All that is known for sure is that Ballew's gun never left its holster. He never had a chance.

Oscar Morgan

Blanchard Police Officer

When Blanchard Police Officer Oscar Morgan joined ranks with the Oklahoma Law Enforcement community his unyielding persistence to track down criminals earned him the nickname "Bloodhound." He was a community hero! In 1920 he rescued a 12-year-old girl who was kidnapped by a farmer. Two years later he assisted in the capture of Arthur Henderson. He was wanted for the murder of W.H. Prewett, a salesman from Oklahoma City. In June of 1924, Morgan was notified of a robbery that took place at the bank at Washington, Oklahoma. Thieves got away with $1,712. He received a tip that the burglars were in the vicinity of the Dibble School House. He parked nearby the school and did an overnight watch, with Night Watchman, Jim Williams by his side. The next day, two men, Guy Wilkerson and Lee McCollum came walking down a dirt road near the school. Sure enough, they seemed to fit the description of the burglars. They drove alongside them and started a conversation. Morgan was in the passenger seat. Wilkerson quickly pulled out his gun and shot at the watchman. The bullet entered the vehicle, ricocheted off the brake and struck Morgan's leg. Just then, McCollum pulled his gun, but before he could fire, Morgan shot over the watchman's shoulder and killed McCollum with a bullet to the temple. They found the stolen money from the bank pinned inside his clothes.

Of all the cases that he solved it would be that of Chester Comer, in 1935, that would cement his name in history as one of Oklahoma's leading lawmen. Before the bloody shootout that dark night between Comer and Morgan, Chester Comer's life was a cloud of mystery. He worked in the oil field and moved about often, hopping from one job to another. At times he went by the name Jack Armstrong. Most Americans living in the country states were hit hard during the Great Depression. They were still climbing out from the damage left behind by the Dust Bowl, so finding work was difficult for many. Comer was one of them.

When he married his first wife, 17-year-old, Elizabeth Childers, he told her family that he was 19 years old, when in fact he was 27 years old. They did not know anything about his past. What they realized later is that shortly after their marriage he became possessive and controlling. He isolated Elizabeth completely from her family. They did not know where he moved her to. They also did not know that after she turned 18 years old, she became pregnant with their first child. Sadly, before the baby was born, Comer murdered her by shooting her five times in the head. He left her buried in a Pauper's Field in Kansas City.

After leaving Kansas, Comer then moved to Oklahoma. In December 1934, just 4 months after he killed Elizabeth, he married his second wife, Lucille Stevens. In November, the following year, she became his second victim. He shot her in the head, as he did to Elizabeth. Two women were now robbed of their lives by this cold-hearted killer. And he was not done yet. After he murdered his second wife he ran. He started hitchhiking across the small towns of Oklahoma. Two days later, just north of Ada, he was picked up by Ray Evans, a prominent attorney from Shawnee. At the time, Evans was leaving a meeting with a client. A few hours later, Evans, was dead. He was only 40 years old. Comer was spotted later that day, north of Maysville, fixing a tire on

Evans' car. The witness stated that Comer had a gun in his pocket and there was a body slumped over in the car. No one is sure what happened in the car that led to his death.

The next day, he kidnapped a family and drove them around all day, terrorizing them. He demanded $3 from the family to be released. Four days later, they found Evans' bloodstained clothes inside his abandoned car. That same day, he was picked up by a farmer and his 15-year-old son, Warren Simpson. They would be his next victims, He shot both of them and left their bodies in a pasture to die. He stole Simpson's car and drove into Blanchard.

When Morgan recognized Simpson's stolen vehicle he attempted to pull him over and a chase pursued. The cars raced at top speed through the rural community when in an instant Comer brought his car to a screeching halt along the edge of a back road. Morgan approached the vehicle and when he reached for the door handle Comer started to shoot at him. As bullets flew through the air one of them struck Morgan's badge, knocking it into the mud. Another bullet tore through Morgan's shoulder. He got wobbly and fell back on his feet, yet managed to fire back. It was dark and raining. Morgan could not see Comer who was ducked down across the front seat. Morgan positioned himself closer to the front of the car and fired two more rounds. It was then that everything fell silent. Officers pulled Comer out of the car, he was barely alive as blood poured from his bullet wounds. One of the bullets from Morgan's gunshot struck Comer between the eyes and burst into 5 fragments. The public found that ironic since Comer killed 5 people. Comer's week-long reign of terror came to an end on November 25, 1935, on the streets of Blanchard, Oklahoma.

As his life was slipping away, the police tried to get Comer to tell him the location of his victim's bodies. He could barely talk and murmured... "Oh, piles of bodies" "east of Fittstown" "Simpson, Simpson was a dirty..." "bodies are all together;" "A pile of bodies in a creek;" "He's down here somewhere." The police desperately wanted Comer to survive so he could tell them where victims' bodies were left. They wanted to know WHY he did all of this, hoping to bring closure for the families of the victims. Those questions would go unanswered. He stopped talking when they reached the hospital, even after they administered truth serum. They even put a variety of objects in his hands to get a response, but nothing. Not until they handed him a pistol. He grasped the gun and pulled the trigger three times. Comer died two days later on Wednesday, November 27, 1935, at 11:09 PM at Oklahoma City hospital. The police embarked on a search for the victims' bodies. By the end of December, the Blanchard police, teamed with neighboring police departments, were able to retrace his steps and find all of the bodies. Including that of his first wife. Her body was returned to her family for a more proper burial.

Dr. D.W. Griffin, of Norman's Central Oklahoma State Hospital, described Comer as "a dangerous type (of person), the type that kills presidents, the type that kills just because he cannot stand to have others around. The victim is like an animal grazing in a green pasture." After Comer's death, they found a business card in one of his pockets with these words scrolled on the back:

"If I am not killed in this car it will be a surprise to me. I have nothing to regret. I had rather be dead than to be a public slave."

Morgan was hospitalized a few days after the death of Comer, due to complications from his shoulder wound. He was never fully healthy after that. Another bullet from the shootout was lodged in his spine. Doctors were unable to remove it. The Pottawatomie County Bar Association awarded Morgan with a $250 gold medal, for Comer's capture. He wore it every single day.

Things did not stay calm for Morgan for long. Three weeks after the shootout and death of Comer, he was called out on a Saturday morning to help locate five escaped convicts. Nothing turned up in his initial search and he went back to patrolling the streets. That very afternoon he found himself in pursuit of a stolen vehicle with two of the convicts inside the car. When the car crossed the Cleveland County line, Officers Phil Eisenhour and H.J. Hilpert joined in the chase to aide Morgan. It was quickly and safely brought to an end and the convicts were captured.

It is said that Morgan was Comer's sixth and final victim. Because of the bullet lodged in his spine, paralysis began to set in after he turned 60 years old. By the time he was 63, he was an invalid. A year later, he was admitted to Oklahoma City General Hospital. He laid under an oxygen tent for several weeks, suffering from double pneumonia and fighting for his life. He died at 64 years old. Upon his death, Morgan was recognized by the Blanchard American Legion, who passed a resolution acknowledging Oscar as Blanchard's most outstanding and most useful citizen. The next morning a story about his death was printed in the Oklahoman newspaper, that started with: "Oscar Morgan, Blanchard's one-man posse, finally lost a fight."

After the shootout, Morgan was invited to Washington DC to meet with F.B.I. Director J. Edgar Hoover. Morgan was also interviewed on national radio, making the people at home in Oklahoma proud of their law officer.

Author's Note: Babe Harmon could have been one of Chester Comer's victims. During Comer's killing spree, Babe gave a ride to a man who looked similar to Comer. He took him into Oklahoma City to pick up a car. He recalled that the man was acting jittery. He would not turn his body to the left and his nervousness gave Babe the impression that he was hiding something. Later, it was scary for Babe to realize how close he came to possibly being one of Comer's victims. If it was him, then he is unsure why Comer would choose to spare his life – unsure, but grateful.

Charles Francis Colcord

Chief of Police

Charles Francis Colcord was a Kentucky native and cousin of abolitionist, Cassius Marcellus Clay first relocated to Kansas in 1876, while traveling with friends to transport

1200 mares to Cherokee territory. While in Kansas, he was a successful farmer, married to Harriet Scoresby. The couple had seven children. Only four of their children survived to adulthood. On April 22, 1889, Colcord participated in the Oklahoma Land Run. When he got there he traded his team and wagon for a shack and a land lot with his lot becoming Lot Number 1, Block Number 1. The next day a tent city had sprung up and Colcord was appointed by the group to lead the makeshift community. This was when Colcord shifted from farming to law enforcement. He started as Oklahoma City's Chief of Police. Two years later, he was elected as Oklahoma City's first Sheriff. From there he made another move to US Marshal. He served under Bill Tilghman for five years. He, alone, caught five members of the Dalton Gang.

After he resigned from law enforcement, Colcord started another farm as a cattle rancher and worked in the oil business. He settled in a town near Delaware County that was just beginning to bloom. The area was named after him - Colcord, Oklahoma. As a prominent businessman, he sat on a number of chairs, including President of the Oklahoma City Chamber of Commerce, President of the Oklahoma Historical Society, the Oklahoma Consistory of the Valley of Guthrie, the Indian Temple, and Ancient Arabic Order of the Nobles of the Mystic Shrine. He achieved the Thirty-Second Degree of the Masonic Order. He also built the Colcord building, which later became the Colcord Hotel. It also became the first skyscraper in Oklahoma City. Colcord was inducted into the Oklahoma Hall of Fame and is considered Oklahoma's First Resident. He died on December 10, 1934. His body lay in state at the Oklahoma Historical Society building. This is the epitaph on his tombstone:

His life was gentle, and the elements
So mix'd in him, that Nature might stand up —
And say to all the world, "This was a man"

Port Lewis

Blanchard Police Department

The history books are filled with stories of Oklahoma's fighting lawmen. Unfortunately, some of the state's notable police officers have not yet received the notoriety they truly deserve. One of Oklahoma's heroes in blue was Port Lewis.

Like the lawmen from the Wild West, Lewis found himself in a shootout in 1950. He was working the night shift when he answered a call for a disturbance at the Texaco Station at Main & Hwy 62. When he arrived he found a husband and wife embroiled in a heated argument. Lewis tried to settle their argument peacefully, but the husband could not be calmed. Lewis grabbed the husband by the arm, fully intending to arrest him at this point. As it happens in most calls like this, the wife then turned on Lewis, berating him and demanding he leave her husband alone. When she then pushed Lewis he released his grip and her husband ran out the door. Lewis did not pursue him because he assumed he ran home. He knew the couple had seven children at home. This was not the case.

A second call came in 20 minutes later about the same couple. The situation had gotten worse. It seems the couple returned and the husband was now armed. He set off the alarm in an attempt to lure Lewis back to that spot. When the alarm sounded, the husband hid in waiting....waiting for Lewis. When Lewis arrived, the drunk husband stepped out and started shooting at him.

Now under a hail of gunfire, both men ducked for cover. The first shot clipped the side of Lewis' hat, grazing a piece of the felt. Another grazed his cheek. As bullets continued to fly through the air, Lewis was shot again. Because he was moving, this bullet went through his chest, cut a button off his shirt and came out behind his left shoulder.

As Lewis lie on the floor bleeding profusely, the shooter was now cursing his gun because it jammed. He wanted to see what was happening with Lewis and when he stepped out, Lewis was able to end the shootout with a fourth shot into one of the legs of the drunk. The owner of the Texaco, Jim Williams, scooped Lewis up off of the floor, put him in his pick-up truck and raced to the hospital. There he learned that his lung was badly injured. Williams was later credited with saving Port Lewis's life.

The wife was there throughout the gun battle and was struck by one of the bullets. The injury left her paralyzed from the waist down for the rest of her life. It remained lodged inside of her for several years. When the bullet worked itself out, it was discovered to be from a 32 handgun. That meant the bullet came from her husband's gun.

The man was never arrested or had to spend one day in jail. Lewis did not want to press charges after hearing him brag that he "wasn't finished with him yet." Lewis was concerned that he would retaliate by going after his children.

Lewis had ten children who meant the world to him. Lewis would take his last breath to defend his family from harm. His children gave him the motivation to pin the metal badge on his chest every morning. And as he lay dying that evening at the service station, it was thoughts of his children that gave him the strength to fight – the strength to survive.

In 1960, Port Lewis started attending services at Blanchard's Trinity Free Holiness Church where his family became friends with the Harmons. They described Port Lewis as a great miracle of the Blanchard Church.

During his days serving in law enforcement, Port was often seen with a cigar in his mouth. In the last 10-12 years of his life, Lewis was famous for driving an old dump truck and doing small jobs for residents. And as he did his days in law enforcement, he was always asking questions.

Justin Terney

Tecumseh Police Officer

The dangers of serving in law enforcement today are just as great as they were in the days of Oscar Morgan. This became all too real for Tecumseh Officer Justin Terney on March 26, 2017. At approximately 11:30 that evening, he pulled over a car being driven by Brooklyn Williams. When he initially pulled her over, her passenger, Byron Shepard, gave Terney a false name claiming to be James Bishop. Terney questioned Shepard when his false identification was revealed. While they were talking, Shepard turned to run off into a wooded area. Terney tasered Shepard but it had no effect. Shepard turned and shot Terney four times. Terney was able to return fire before falling from his wounds. Terney died a few hours later on March 27th, from his gunshot wounds. Officer Terney was only 22 years old and had only been a police officer for a year. To honor his service, on November 15, 2017, signs were unveiled to the public to name a 4-mile section of US 177 "Officer Justin Terney Memorial Highway."

Author Notes: On the third floor of the Oklahoma History Museum is a section set out for Oklahoma Law Enforcement. The complex is located in the State Capitol Complex in Oklahoma City on 800 Nazih Auhdi Drive. Richard Boyd, Secretary of the Museum, explained, "we do have a lot of law enforcement pieces that represent our history since the days of 'Indian Territory' and the US Marshal's who kept the peace there. We also have a kiosk featuring Oklahoma law enforcement people who have been inducted into the HOF since 2009." The rich history told inside the museum makes it a must-have visit!

Did You Know?

The first Oklahoma Police Officer to die in the line of duty was Deputy Sheriff David Cox. On Friday, January 31, 1908, Cox was shot in the chest attempting to arrest the owner of a shooting gallery after receiving a complaint about illegal weapons at the gallery. He is buried at Glory Cemetery in Hughes County, Oklahoma.

On Tuesday, August 27, 1996, Rita K. Duncan became the first Oklahoma woman to be elected sheriff.

Judge Isaac Parker was nicknamed "the hanging judge" because he condemned more people to death by hanging than any judge in history.

Native American Peace Officers were called "Lighthorse Officers."

There have been 506 Law Enforcement Officers killed in Oklahoma's history. The Officers Down Memorial Page lists there deaths as:

Animal related 1
Assault 15
Automobile crash 40
Drowned 2
Duty related illness 2
Explosion 1
Gunfire 339
Gunfire (Accidental) 17
Heart attack 13
Motorcycle crash 8
Stabbed 6
Struck by train 4
Struck by vehicle 12
Training accident 1
Vehicle pursuit 19
Vehicular assault 17
Weather/Natural disaster 1

Bass Reeves is a Wild West legend whose life was tragically cut short from Bright's Disease

Bill Tilghman was a criminal as a young man. He turned his life around then accepted a job as a US Marshal in Dodge City in 1884.

The Three Guardsmen: Heck Thomas, Chris Madsen, and
Bill Tilghman

James Franklin "Bud" Ledbetter was often called "the fourth
horseman."

E.D. Nix was cheated out of his law enforcement career by a clerical error.

Frank Canton lived a life of secrecy to hide from the crimes he committed as a young man. When he confessed his actions to accept his punishment, he was absolved of all wrongdoing. They considered his career as a dedicated lawman to be proof that he turned his life around for the better.

A display of Stringer Fenton showcased inside the Guthrie Territorial Museum.

Oscar Morgan earned the nickname "Bloodhound" for his amazing ability to track down criminals.

Deputy Bud Ballew shaking hands with Sheriff Buck Garrett

Bill Tilghman and Charles Colcord at the opening of the
Cherokee Strip in Oklahoma.

George Ransom's Saloon, the site of a gun battle between the US Marshals and members of the Doolin-Dalton gang. "Arkansas Tom" Jones was on the second floor at the Ingalls hotel when he heard the gun battle outside his window. It was from there that he shot and killed US Deputy Marshal Thomas Houston.

Dode Lewis and Officer Port Lewis are remembered as a sweet and endearing couple. Port is known for his amazing bravery, compassion for life, and dedication to his community

Officer Justin Terney died a hero at the young age of 22 years old.

Port Lewis riding a bronco at the 1946 Blanchard rodeo. The rodeo and horses were provided by the Giles ranch. Immediately after this photo was taken, the horse ran through the fence. He made a complete circle, then came back into the arena through the same hole in the fence. Port stayed on top of the bronco throughout the whole wild ride!

Tony Burris is one of the men sitting on a gate in the background. He later gave his life on a battlefield in Korea. He died, defending the lives of others.

Cecil Harmon is also in the background. He is standing fifth from the right, wearing overalls and rolling a Prince Albert cigarette.

Also in the photo is Max Williams, Jack Byers, Truman Ellard (owner of the Ritz theatre in Blanchard), Bobby Harmon, Amos Sailors, and Pate Lewis (Port's brother).

Chapter 7

Growing Up In Oklahoma

Kenny and Jon may not have had many toys but they always had many things to do. After a good rain, they would walk to the large culvert, that was about a 1/8 mile west of their grandmother's house. Culverts were concrete tunnels built to channel the water flow away from the highway above it. The stream that ran through the culvert was a peaceful world for minnows and small fish (Perch and Mud Cats), Crawdads (Crayfish), turtles, and snakes. Kenny used to fish for crawdads using a stick and a piece of string that had chunks of bacon tied at the end. The crawdads were attracted to the smell of bacon and would use their claws to clutch on to it. The fun took a turn for the worse during one afternoon. Kenny was walking through, wearing a pair of tennis shoes, that had holes in the toes. He spotted a water snake in the mud and went to step on his head. Instead, he stepped on the snake's back. This enabled the snake to turn his head and scratch one of his toes with his teeth. Suddenly, to Kenny, that harmless water snake turned to a deadly water moccasin. He took off running for home. He crashed through the front door and ran to his mother to announce that he could die from all of this. She examined the bite and calmed Kenny down by explaining the "teeth marks" were just scratches.

That would not have been Kenny's first trip to the hospital. The family doctor that mended most of his injuries was Doc Holcomb. The first time happened when he was five years old and he wrecked his bike into a 3 foot ditch. When he was nine years old, he had a boil on his eyebrow that had to be lanced. The boil was an infected lump under the skin caused by an infected hair follicle.

He was not a stranger to getting stitches either. As a child, he was at home, in the potato house, and got a gash on his foot when he was playing with an ax.

Growing up, Kenny had a few scares that stayed with him for years. Kenny was stubborn in his way of thinking, so much so, that even at a young age once a thought entered his mind, it took hold and nothing, absolutely nothing, could change his way of thinking. One of the experiences that stayed with him was when he was riding a neighbor's Shetland Pony. Somehow the pony got spooked and took Kenny on a short wild ride - straight into a fence. Kenny did not have any experience on the horse and he thought it was going to try and jump the fence. The horse came to a sudden stop, which sent Kenny flying through the air. It knocked the breath out of him. Having a complete inability to get your lungs to work can be scary for an adult, let alone for a child. With Kenny, that memory stayed with him in the worst way. He never rode a horse again.

One of the biggest years in Kenny's childhood was 1957. This was the year he began working on the family farm. It was his first real job and he was excited to have it. But that was just the first big change. He was hoping to one day save up enough money for a Daisy BB gun. His mother and Uncle Gaylon had a suggestion to help him with his goal. The two were planning to spend the afternoon picking cotton and invited Kenny to join them. He was happy to join them; he wanted that gun so dearly. Wanda told Kenny that he can either pick cotton or pull bolls. Pulling bolls means to open the flower of the plant that has not yet exposed the cotton. Kenny will never forget the rewards from that work. "It was a hard day but it was worth it, I got my first gun!" He was a dollar short on the money needed but Gaylon gave him enough to finish the costs, (about $9). Gaylon was more like a big brother than an uncle. He took that Daisy BB gun on his first hunting trips for birds. He kept a notebook where he wrote the type of bird he shot and how many of each.

Author's Notes: The Daisy BB Gun was first created in 1888 by Clarence Hamilton. He brought it to the Plymouth Iron Windmill Company to see if they would be interested in producing it. When General Manager Lewis Hough tested the gun he excitedly shouted, "Boy, it's a daisy!" hence branding the name, the Daisy BB Gun.By 1895, the gun had gained such notoriety for the company that they stopped making windmills to focus solely on guns. The company name was also changed to the Daisy Manufacturing Company.

Kenny soon wanted something bigger, something he could use to hunt rabbits, crows and hawks. Like generations of Harmon men before him, Kenny got his first "real gun" when he was 9 years old. It was all he hoped and prayed for the whole year. Sure enough on Christmas morning there it was under the tree – the 22. rifle he wanted so much. He would always remember his brother, John, happily shouting, "Wow, Kenny, it's a gun!" He also remembers the first crow he shot with that rifle. It was pretty exciting for him! Crows were some of the worst pests on the farm, especially for their watermelon.

After two years, Kenny grew bored with the rifle and longed for a gun with more power. His mom rewarded him with a gift of a Remington 5 shot 20 gauge shotgun. The shotgun was the last gun of his youth. It was a versatile gun and great for hunting rabbits, quails, crows, and hawks. The most significant kill for his shotgun was in the fall of '65. It was a Saturday morning, not long after sunrise, he heard a commotion from the south side of the house near the front door where the puppies were kept. They were making terrible sounds. A few seconds later his mother burst into his bedroom yelling, "Kenny there's a skunk attacking the puppies." He knew the skunk was rabid because skunks are never seen out in the daylight. And a skunk would only attack a dog if it was rabid.

Kenny jumped out of bed, threw on his clothes and grabbed his shotgun. He slid in a couple shells and darted out the back door. He wanted at least two shots and he needed to get the skunk off the porch. When he came around the side of the house, the skunk was too busy with the puppies to notice Kenny. He wanted to lure the skunk away so he did not accidentally shoot the house or the car. When he got in position, approximately 15 feet from the porch, he aimed his gun and hollered to get the skunk's attention. The skunk immediately made contact with Kenny, he leaped from the porch to charge toward Kenny, which is what he expected and wanted him to do. As soon as his feet hit the ground he was dead. It took one shot and it was over.

Kenny and Wanda took the skunk into Purcell to have it examined. Since the skunk came in contact with the puppies they needed to know for sure if it was rabid. While they were away, Wanda told the girls not to touch the puppies. When they got back home all three of the girls were indeed playing with the puppies. That was it, Rhonda, Debbie, and Donna now had to get a shot for rabies by Doc Holcomb, an old school doctor. On their way to Blanchard, Rhonda and Debbie were making fun of Donna, telling her it would be a long needle and how much it would hurt. By the time Wanda arrived at Doc Holcomb's, Donna was so scared that they had to hold her down to give her the shot. But, their scare tactics were about to backfire. Since Donna was so frightened of the needle, Doc Holcomb gave her the shot first. Unfortunately, he used the same needle on all three of them. It was not considered dangerous at that time but it was. Reusing the same needle caused an infection to spread. Since Donna was first to get the shot, she did not get sick. Debbie was second to get the shot, so she had a little swelling at the injection sight. Rhonda was third to get the shot, so the infection was worse for her. The spot on her stomach, where she received the shot was swollen and painful.

Less than two months after the skunk incident there was another drama filled night at their house. It was not long after dark when a close friend of his parents showed up at their house to escape her drunk husband. Kenny went to his room to get away from the emotional talk. Less than an hour later, the drunk husband also showed up. She went outside to talk to him, in hopes of calming him down. He threatened her with a knife saying she would come home with her or else. His parents tried to intervene and he turned on them. When Kenny realized his parents were in danger he loaded up his 20 gauge shotgun and went to the door to watch what was happening. He was not about to let anyone hurt his parents in their own front yard. After 15 minutes the husband calmed down and they left without anyone getting hurt. Kenny was glad that it ended that way. He did not want to have to shoot someone. That's quite a lot for a 15-year-old boy.

When the family got their first TV, his favorite shows were the Lone Ranger, the Three Stooges, and Superman (with George Reeves). Though he had a great time watching TV at home with his family, nothing meant more to him than the time he spent at his grandparent's house.

Through the years, Kenny spent countless hours at the home of his grandparents, Nellie and Babe. He visited them nearly every day. His grandmother always had a treat made for him, so going to see what she cooked for him was one of his highlights. Some of those snacks included cinnamon toast and fried chicken. His favorite treat of all was the homemade ice cream. He did not know how she made it but it was prepared using the metal ice cube trays.

Nellie made popcorn every night for Babe; which Kenny also enjoyed. He especially liked the leftover popcorn from the night before. Kenny and Babe watched westerns, such as Bonanza, Rawhide, and Maverick. Bonanza, Babe's favorite show, holds the record as NBC's longest running western. The show aired for 14 years.

On Fridays they watched the Gillette Cavalcade of Sports, also called the Friday Night Fights. The show aired from 1954 – 1960. Before the fights, Sharpie, the station's parrot, would squawk, "Look Sharp, Be Sharp with Gillette Razor Blades." Then it was time to watch the best of the 50's, Sugar Ray Robinson, Gene Fulmer, Carmen Basilio, Jersey Joe Walcott, Ezzard Charles, and the biggest name of the 50's - Rocky Marciano. In May 1953, it was only $50 for a ticket to watch a heavyweight championship fight live between Marciano vs Walcott.

One evening after he left their house it was dark and something in the shadows startled him and he took off running down the driveway and crashed right into a plow. He smacked off of it and fell to the ground. He could not get back up to walk and had to crawl 50 yards home. He was left with a pretty big bruise and a dent in his left thigh.

Kenny was protective of the attention and snacks that he got at his grandparent's house. When he became a teenager, he spent less and less time there and more time out with his friends. The void he left was quickly filled by his younger sister, Donna. One afternoon, Babe was teaching Donna and her friend, Kathy Taylor, how to spit watermelon seeds. Nellie did not like to see the young girls practicing spitting distance and scolded Babe not to teach them such things. As soon as she went back to the house the lesson continued. Babe told the girls that "it's all about holding your head back, wrinkling your nose, and giving it all you got!" Kenny had a great bond with Babe and Nellie. Now his little sister was getting the opportunity to form just as strong a bond.

Kenny and his friends were pretty unpredictable. Hanging out with friends at Hub & Lil's Diner in Blanchard was another favorite spot. Summer carnivals were always fun! Except for the time that he and his friend, Butch Ladd, decided to participate in a boxing match. Being friends, they just wanted to have fun. They agreed they would not hit each other in the face. Once in the ring, standing face-to-face, Kenny could tell that something changed with Butch. A dark look came across his face, maybe from the heat of the moment. Before Kenny could react, Butch punched him cold in the nose. As blood streamed down his face, Butch panicked and apologized. Kenny knew he was genuinely sorry for what he did.

In school, Kenny was a well-behaved student who gave his best, though his first day got off to a rocky start. He did not go to kindergarten and he was terrified on his first day of grade grade. He was throwing a tantrum about having to go to school. His mother offered him a dime to buy candy from York's store if he would go to class. He threw the dime in the grass hoping she would feel bad and take him back home. That did not work. When she drove off he tried to find the dime but never did. After he settled down to the idea of going to school, Kenny approached school like he approached everything in life – sports, farming, hunting – he gave it his all. In grade school he was highly intelligent and made exceptional grades. He was extremely neat and kept his papers organized. However, his behavior was quite erratic. His attitude depended on his feelings about the teachers. If he liked a teacher, he caused fewer problems, if any.

Some of his favorite teachers were Mrs. Gilmore, from second grade, Mrs. Hayhurst, from third grade, and Mrs. Harmon (no relation to him) from fifth grade. In high school, Kenny was a part of Future Farmers of America (FFA). Jerry Mayfield taught that course. He started teaching at Dibble High School during Kenny's freshman year. He taught the course for many years and became one of the most liked and respected teachers in the history of Dibble High School. Mayfield was a quiet man but could be a stickler with the students. Kenny learned, the hard way, just how stern Mayfield could be when students got out of line. During an afternoon when Kenny's mouth landed him in trouble, he found himself in the hall getting paddled by Mayfield. After two swats, Kenny learned not to act that way with Mayfield anymore. Elwood Ladd was another favorite of Kenny's. Ladd taught Auto Mechanics. Joe Work was his high school baseball and basketball coach. Work was a man of few words. He earned the students respect without having to say much. His wife taught English and had the same personality.

Kenny's first car was a '57 Bel Air. This car was his dating wagon, a hangout spot, and a stunt vehicle on back roads. When he and his friends were riding around town they munched on bags of sunflower seeds. They used to spit the hulls into the floorboard. After a year of spitting the hulls, the floorboards were ½" deep in sunflower hulls.

One of the worst experiences of Kenny's school years happened on a fall night in 1962. He was in 7th grade, at the time. His friend, Richard Hurd was visiting Kenny and stayed pretty late into the night. It was a cool foggy evening and it was dark when Richard left to go home. He lived nearly 4 miles north of the Dibble CrossRoads (Junction Highways 39 and 76), off Highway 76. He was less than a mile away from home when he was struck by a car and killed. Kenny was already heartbroken having lost his good friend but the next morning when he stepped on the school bus, one of the high school students shouted out in an angry tone, "Why did you let Richard leave your house?" Kenny was stunned! How could anyone ask such a cruel question? He had no answer for him. Kenny was only a child, himself. There was not anything he could have done to change the events of that night. Walking home, even 4 miles, was not uncommon. No one could have predicted that Richard was at risk of getting hit by a car. The callous question was unnecessary.

Rock & Roll

Like most teenagers, Kenny was a rock & roll fan, still is! Many people believe that Cleveland Disc Jockey, Alan Freed, coined the phrase "rock & roll." Those people would be wrong. The fact is, the expression was used in the 1930's. In 1934, the Boswell Sisters even did a song titled, "Rock and Roll." Freed first heard the expression in 1952 when he was visiting a record store owned by Leo Mintz. There he learned that Leo used the expression "rock & roll" as a way to promote his albums. We may never know who truly coined the phrase "rock & roll" what we do know is that Freed popularized it on his radio show.

The 50's are the foundation of rock & roll music but the 60's brought in a whirlwind of changes, that especially includes the rock n' roll fans in Oklahoma. Some of the pioneers of rock & roll from the 50's were the Everly Brothers, Buddy Holly, Chuck Berry, Little Richard and Jerry Lee Lewis. The 1960's escorted in great bands, including the Byrds, Van Morrison, Dave Clark Five, and the most popular one of all, the Beatles. The Rolling Stones debuted in 1962. The Beatles arrived in America on February 7, 1964. With the arrival of Beatlemania, a surge of rock bands grew across the country. The Ventures helped shape the direction that rock and roll music was taking. They are known as "the band that launched a thousand bands." The Ventures was founded by Bob Bogle and Don Wilson. Bogle was born and raised in Wagoner, Oklahoma.

Small rock bands were popping up in Oklahoma that imitated these great stars. One of Dibble's hometown favorites was the Teen Beats. Butch Ladd was the lead singer and guitarist. Jimmy Anderson was also on guitar. The backup singers Steve Walker and Bob Walker. Of all the music Kenny listened to, the Teen Beats was one of his favorites.

The Teen Beats played at parties and in community events. They brought the nations favorite rock & roll tunes to center stage for the teens in Blanchard. Some of the most requested songs were hits by Dave Clark Five, such as, "Because" and "Can't You See That She's Mine." They also played Van Morrison's hits "Gloria," and "Here Comes the Night." Van Morrison's first band was "Them." He went on as a solo performer in 1967. Kenny also remembers the Teen Beats performing these fan favorites:

I Fought the Law by the Bobby Fuller Four

Game of Love by Wayne Fontana and the Mind Benders

I Used to Love Her by the Rolling Stones

Jolly Green Giant by the Kingsmen

Walking the Dog by Mitch Ryder and the Detroit Wheels

There were a number of musicians and songwriters that came out of Oklahoma. That includes Shelby "Sheb" Wooley, singer of Purple People Eater, who was from Erick, Oklahoma. Then there was Neal Schon, lead guitarist for Journey. When he was 15 years old Eric Clapton invited Neal to join Derek and the Dominos. He was also invited to join Santana. He chose to play for Santana. Also, Billy Joe Thomas, of Hugo, Oklahoma will forever be remembered for his song, "Raindrops Keep Fallin' on My Head."

Songwriter Hoyt Axton was born in Duncan, Oklahoma, and raised in Comanche. He wrote "Joy to the World" for Three Dog Night and several songs for Joan Baez, Waylon

Jennings, John Denver, Linda, Ronstadt, and Elvis Presley. His mother, Mae Boren Axton, co-wrote Presley's song "Heartbreak Hotel." It went on to become his first #1 hit! Axton left Oklahoma in April 1956 when he found himself in trouble. He participated in a practical joke that went wrong, causing Knauer's Hardware Store on Myrtle Avenue to burn down.

A number of Country singers also call Oklahoma their home state. Those famed country stars include Vince Gill (Norman), Toby Keith (Clinton), Mel McDaniel (Checotah), Blake Shelton (Ada), and Reba McEntire (McAlester). The biggest name in country music to come from Oklahoma was Troyal Garth Brooks. Garth was born and raised in Tulsa Oklahoma. His parents Troyal and Colleen used to hold family talent nights, encouraging their children to sing and dance. David Gates was also from Tulsa. David was a 70's sensation, as the co-leader of Bread.

Girls! Girls! Girls! (And the one that got away)

For Kenny, the next best thing to Oklahoma sports were the Oklahoma girls. Kenny boasts about how Blanchard and Dibble were full of beautiful girls. "I would match that area anywhere with beautiful young ladies," bragged Kenny. When he was 15 years old, he was sitting in the family car outside Harold's Dairy Land when a super cute girl stepped out of the burger restaurant and caught his eye. The girl's name was Rhonda. His first thought was, "She's cute, but she has an attitude."

Some of the most attractive girls were Melba, Kay, Ann, Linda, Shirley, and Jean. But it was Joetta Whitford that was the first to win his heart. She had smooth dark hair that stopped short at her shoulders. He was 15 years old when he met her and would always describe her as "very attractive." It was around that time that he was taking trips into Blanchard on Friday nights to watch high school football games. He met Joetta at one of those games. The day started with a trip into town with his friends, John Clift, James DeWoody and Jerry Price. By the end of the day, he was at his first live football game and falling head-over-heels for Joetta.

A few months later, in January 1966, Kenny received his driver's license. The first thing he did was to immediately ask Joetta to the Blanchard dance. The Teen Beats would be playing there. This was it, that Saturday night would be his first REAL date – picking her up in his car, driving her home at the end of the night – it would be perfect. Well, it did not work out the way he thought.

Kenny's family only had one car. His mother was running late and was not going to be on time for Kenny to get the car for his date. It never occurred to him to call Joetta and let her know. A big rookie mistake. He just waited nervously and watched each minute pass by on the clock. For Joetta, those minutes were just as tense. Thinking that Kenny was standing her up, she and her friend decided to go to the dance without him. When he pulled up to her house, he was 20 minutes late and his date was gone.

He immediately went to the dance and saw his beautiful date wearing a pretty blue dress. But she was furious with Kenny and would not talk to him at all. He felt like a heel. He certainly did not want to dance with anyone else there. They rarely spoke after that night. It drove him crazy knowing that he ruined their one and only date and one phone call from him could have changed everything. He still wonders "what if?"

A few weeks after the dance, he was in Auto Mechanics class when he was informed by the teacher, Mr. Ladd (Butch Ladd's father), that he had a call. He walked nervously to the phone, hoping that nothing was wrong. The voice on the other end was a girl claiming to be Joetta. Kenny knew the whole time that it was not her, but her best friend Sharon Spoon. He played along anyway.

High school was just the beginning and Kenny was clueless of the things to come. By January 1966, Kenny would exit his previous life of caution and careful as he entered life's fast lane. Similar to the "Prodigal Son" Kenny would become reckless and carefree. However in Kenny's future there would be an awakening!

Did you know?

Skunks are immune to snake venom.

The Recording Industry Association of America lists Garth Brooks as the Best Selling American Artist in history. Yes, he outsold Elvis Presley. Garth's sales come in second only to the Beatles.

In the movie, "The Claw," there is a scene early in the film that shows panicked crowds running away. That footage was taken from the movie "The Day the Earth Stood Still."

Today there are six drive-ins still open in Oklahoma. They are the Admiral Twin in Tulsa, the Beacon in Guthrie, the Chief in Chickasha, the Corral in Guymon, the Tower in Poteau and the Winchester in Oklahoma City.

According to Mental Floss magazine, Paul Newman met with West Virginians to learn their accent. He spent a weekend in Huntington, West Virginia, with businessman, Andy Houvouras, on a recommendation of a friend. Houvouras drove him to several counties where he talked to residents and recorded them.

Some of the faculty at Dibble School District, including a few
of Kenny's favorites.

Joetta Whitford was Kenny's first crush. The girl that left him
wondering.....what if?

Kenny Harmon, at 2-years-old, had a charming smile.

Donna Harmon in 1966, sitting on the hood of Kenny's first car, a '57 Bel Air.

Kenny Harmon's Elementary School Years

First Grade

Second Grade

Third Grade

Ruby Jones, Jake Jones SR, and Johnny Jones SR, in 1932, outside the Ritz in downtown Shawnee, Oklahoma.

Debbie, Kenny, Jon, and Rhonda at Kenny's 9th birthday party on January 12, 1959.

Dibble Crossroads Store before Highways 76 & 39 were built. The store was owned by Buzz and Mable Harmon.

The Shawnee Fire Department brought their fire trucks to display in front of the Cozy Theatre in honor of "The Fire Brigade" that was playing inside the theatre.

Nellie Harmon in 1969, after Babe passed away. She
seemed to appear so sad.

An ad from the Ritz in June 1961.

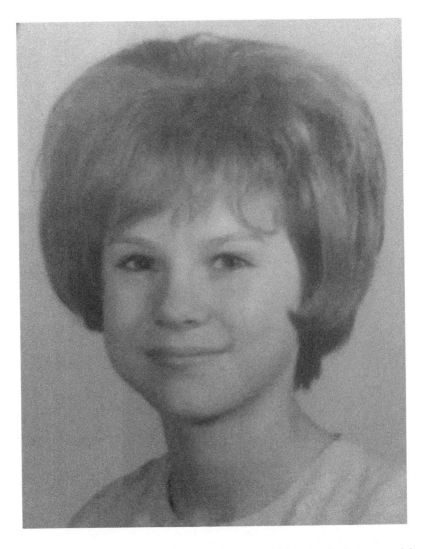

Thirteen-year-old Rhonda Curren in 1965. This is how old she was when 15-year old Kenny Harmon first saw her outside Harold's Dairy Land diner.

An old ad by Hub & Lil's, a small diner that Kenny and his friends often went to when they were teens.

George, Floetta, Gary and Glen Moore having lots of family fun!

Jon, Debbie, and Rhonda Harmon in 1957.

Jon Harmon in 1958. He was in first grade.

Rhonda Harmon in 1956 at Spring Lake Park in Chickasha.

September 1950 ~ Paula Swinney and Nedra Swinney
holding baby Kenny Harmon.

The Royal Theatre in Pauls Valley, 1960. It was here that Kenny went to see The Claw and I was a Teenage Frankenstein.

A photo taken at Dibble carnival the year that Butch Ladd and Kenny Harmon had their boxing match. In this photo is Becky Ward, Wayne Green, Joyce Keeler, and Dale Roath. Kenny Harmon is in the background, over Joyce Keeler's shoulder.

Sixteen-year-old Rhonda Curren.

Eighteen year old Kenny Harmon in 1968. It was at this time that he started dating Rhonda Curren.

Chapter 8

Tragedy on the Home Front

On Thursday, August 12, 1965, darkness would once again loom over the Harmon family. The day started off great! Kenny's favorite cousin, Glen, was there for a visit. Glen, Kenny, and his brother, Jon, spent the morning picking watermelons. That might sound simple but imagine picking Jubilee watermelons from 5 acres of farmland – that is 217,800 square feet! But to country boys who grew up farming that was fun...hard, but fun!

When the work was done, Glen and Jon left to walk to the Dibble Crossroads Store. It was less than a ½ mile walk from their home. As they walked along the edge of Highway 39, Jon attempted to cross the highway, just as a car approached from the west. The driver saw the boys and honked his horn to get their attention. Jon hollered to Glen, "Watch this." Those were his last words. He ran directly in front of the approaching car. The driver's only recourse was to slam on the brakes. Investigators later determined that the speed of the car upon impact was nearly 45 MPH. There was nothing the driver could have done to stop the events of the accident.

Glen was walking ahead of Jon and did not realize that he decided to cross the highway until he heard the screeching brakes and the crashing sounds of Jon being struck by the car. He turned quickly to see his cousin lying on the side of the road, fighting for his life. The driver was traumatized at what just happened. Jon lived for less than an hour.

Kenny was at home when his grandfather and Uncle Kenneth approached him with the news of his brother's death. It was the first time Kenny saw his grandfather break down in tears. At Jon's funeral, there was not a dry eye in the house. This was Kenny's first funeral and it instilled a fear of funerals in him. As broken as Kenny and his sisters felt, there was no pain comparable to what Billy and Wanda felt. The death of their son put an ache in their soul that nothing on Earth can heal. Not a holiday would go by without them thinking of Jon. There would never be another "happy birthday" for Jon and the day of his death would forever loom over them like a dark cloud. When your child dies it feels like time stopped at that moment they took their last breath. The Harmon family was always a close-knit group and it would be that closeness, that bond, that strong support of love that would help Billy and Wanda to carry on, even on the days that just getting out of bed would be a struggle.

Jon lived 13 short years in this world. In that time he brought happiness to all he met. He was rambunctious, much like his dad was as a boy. But most of the time he got into trouble he was only trying to help. Like the time he was working on fence posts, got injured and found himself in the hospital getting stitches. At five years old, he decided to give Kenny's chicken, Pete, a bath in a mud hole when it accidentally drown. He carried Pete to the kitchen and put him in a propane stove in an attempt to dry him off and revive him.

When he was seven years old he accidentally set the kitchen on fire. The family used to burn the garbage behind their 3-room house. On this day, as their mother was leaving the house she instructed Jon to burn the garbage. Their sister, Rhonda, watched as Jon proceeded to pile the garbage on the kitchen floor. He struck a match and tossed it onto the garbage pile as his mother instructed. Luckily, Rhonda and Jon remembered the water bucket nearby and quickly put out the fire. He was a fun loving and carefree boy. His last carefree thought ended his life.

There was a big change in the Harmon family after Jon's death. The following month, Nellie had a new ride to church on Sundays...her husband, Babe. He walked side-by-side with Nellie through the doors of the Blanchard Free Holiness Church. He was 77 years old when Jesus entered his heart. It was not just Babe by her side. In fact, the church had grown by seven new members. Billy, Wanda, Kenny, Rhonda, Debbie, and Donna, would also accompany them that day and every week after that. Nellie always hoped that her family would join her at church. Though, this was not how she wanted that to happen. The family still attends the Blanchard Free Holiness Church to this day.

The Harmon family found comfort in the words that "God works in mysterious ways." They also now had a new wall of emotional support that came through their new "church family." They knew they would see Jon again one day. Until that day comes, they released their grief in God's hands so that Jon can rest in peace.

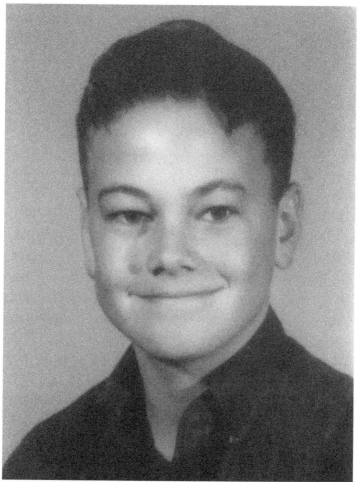

Jon Harmon at the age of 13 years old. This photograph was taken four months before he died.

The Sad Papaw Books

Kenny Harmon has lived a life full of the ups and downs that many of us face. There was dating, friends, family, and high school fun, along with facing fears, broken relationships, and financial struggles. He also saw the dark side of life, the death of a brother, then the death of a friend, and backbreaking work as a teenager. Those trials, all the good and the bad, shaped the man he is today. A hardworking man who loves his family; practices his faith, and honors our soldiers. The man who today is known around the world as Sad Papaw has chosen to share his life with the rest of us. As we all wondered who is the man behind the sad tweet, he now regales us with what life taught him and what he can now teach us. Starting with the importance of family. As you close book number two, know that he has much more to share with us as the Sad Papaw series continues.

Celebrating 46

When Oklahoma earned statehood into America they became the nation's 46th state. In honor of Oklahoma's history, we celebrate 46!

46 Fun Facts about Oklahoma

1) The name "Oklahoma" was suggested by a Choctaw Chief. It was derived from two Choctaw words, "okla" and "humma," meaning "red people." He chose those words because he hoped that the area would one day be a Native American state. Before deciding on the name "Oklahoma," they considered the names Indiahoma and Indianola.

2) Carl Magee, of Oklahoma City, is credited for inventing the parking meter. On May 13, 1935, he filed his patent for the "coin controlled parking meter" The first parking meter was installed in Oklahoma City on July 16, 1935.

3) Vinita is the first town in Oklahoma to have electricity. The town was first named Downingville. It was later changed to honor Vinnie Ream, the sculptress who created the life-size statue of Abraham Lincoln at the United States Capitol.

4) A married couple was at home in Ponca City when a tornado swept through, lifting their home up from the ground. The high winds ripped off the walls and the roof. The couple clung together, as the floor or the house carried them further down the road and set them back on the ground, unharmed.

5) Guthrie was made the first capitol of Oklahoma in 1907. In 1910, residents voted in a special election to change the capitol to Oklahoma City.

6) The town of Beaver is the Cow Chip Throwing Capital of the World. Every year in April, they hold the World Championship Cow Chip Throw.

7) Sylvan Goldman, owner of the Humpty Dumpty supermarket chain in Oklahoma City invented the shopping cart in 1940.

8) The University of Central Oklahoma opened on December 24, 1890. It was Oklahoma's first school of higher education. It was originally titled the Territorial Normal School and was a college for teachers. There were 23 students in the first class that met in November 1891. Today there are 17,000 students. They were on the list of America's Best Colleges.

9) Foress B. Lillie entered Oklahoma during the Land Run of 1889. That day, he set up a tent and was open for business as a pharmacy. His store, Lillie's Drug, located in Guthrie, was issued the No. 1 license certificate and became the first drug store in the state of Oklahoma.

10) There is a statue claiming to be the world's largest peanut was erected on November 15, 1974, in Durant. It is dedicated to the Peanut Growers in Bryan County.

11) Christmas was illegal in Oklahoma until 1907. Tattoos were illegal until 1963.

12) When Eric James Torpy was sentenced to 30 years for shooting with an intent to kill and robbery, he asked for his sentence to be increased to 33 years to match Larry Bird's jersey number.

13) Deer were once a rare animal in Oklahoma. In fact, the first animal in the Oklahoma Zoo was a fawn that was donated. Visitors flocked to see the deer that they thought for sure would soon be extinct.

14) The town of Hydro was founded in 1901. That year they had their first Free Fair – the Hydro Fair! To this day, they have never let a summer go by without holding their free fair.

15) Kingfisher has always been the largest wheat market in America, earning them the name, "Buckle of the Wheat Belt."

16) Clinton Riggs designed the YIELD sign. It was first used on a trial basis in Tulsa. It was originally read as "Yield Right of Way."

17) George Steele, of Indiana, was the first Governor of Oklahoma Territory. He was not elected. He was appointed by President Harrison in 1890.

18) During the Presidential election of 1916, over 45,000 Oklahoma residents voted for the Socialist party.

19) During the Triassic Period, Oklahoma was actually located near the equator.

20) Gordon Matthews who was born and raised in Tulsa, Oklahoma, invented the answering machine in 1982.

21) Ed Malzahn invented the Ditch Witch, a trencher used when installing underground utilities. Fortune magazine named the Ditch Witch one of the 100 best American-made products in the world.

22) Oklahoma's Poteau River is the only river in Oklahoma that flows north. No one knows why.

23) The original Dibble Post Office was discontinued in 1926. In was reinstated in 1953. At that time a stamp was only 3 cents.

24) Through time, Oklahoma has had its share of firsts. In Bartlesville Oklahoma, a new library was built. And what made it significant? It was the first time a building was used solely as a library. Before that, libraries shared a space inside a building with numerous other businesses.

25) Until 1933, Oklahoma was a dry state. It was not legal to sell hard liquor until 1959.

26) The House of Representatives voted watermelon as the official state vegetable of Oklahoma. (Yes, it is a fruit AND a vegetable.)

27) Edward Roberts, a graduate of Oklahoma State University, the Altair 8800 personal computer. It was the first commercially sold computer. In fact, he coined the words "personal computer." Roberts also gave Bill Gates his first job working in computers.

28) Blanchard was once a part of Chickasha. They were established as their own community on October 25, 1907.

29) There are several authors from Oklahoma. Here are just a few.

Angie Debo (Oklahoma historian)
William Bernhardt (The Ben Kincaid series)
Louis L'Amour (Western novels and historical fiction)
Tracy Letts (Who's Afraid of Virginia Wolf)
Tony Hillerman (The Navajo Tribal Police mystery novels)
S.E. Hinton (The Outsiders)
Edward Gaylord (Editor/founder of the Daily Oklahoman)

30) Blake Edwards, of Tulsa, created the Pink Panther cartoon in 1963. Did you know that in 1973 Post introduced Pink Panther Flakes? It was sweet pink flakes that also turned the milk pink.

31) The first Tornado Warning was exercised on March 25, 1948, in Oklahoma City. It was shortly before a tornado touched down but thanks to their new warning system, no lives were lost.

32) The Chipachawamie tribe was supposed to be included in the Trail of Tears but they died of famine before it.

33) Olivia Jordan, of Tulsa, was voted Miss USA in 2015. She was second-runner up in the Miss Universe Pageant that same year.

34) Businessmen Sherman Billingsly (The Stork Club), Sam Walton (Wal-Mart), David Green (Hobby Lobby), and Troy Smith (Sonic) all call Oklahoma home. Billingsly is from Enid. Walton is from Kingfisher. Green and Smith are both from Oklahoma City.

35) On June 27, 1994, temperatures in Tipton reached 120 degrees, the highest ever in Oklahoma history. The lowest temperature was -27 degrees, recorded in Vinita on February 13, 1905, and again in Watts on January 18, 1930.

36) Clarence Nash, of Watonga, was the original voice for Donald Duck. In Finnish when voters want to protest an election, they mark their ballots with the name Donald Duck.

37) Bub Dunn, of Braggs Oklahoma, invented the electric guitar in 1935. He was added to the Steel Guitar Hall of Fame in 1992.

38) Braum's Dairy, in Tuttle, produces more than one million glasses of milk every day.

39) Native American Maria Tallchief, of Fairfax, was America's first Prima Ballerina.

40) ESPN named Oklahoma University "the most prestigious college football program in modern college football."

41) Aviator, Wiley Post, of Maysville, created the pressurized suit in 1934. He was concerned about getting sick on a flight. He was certain that his 3-layered suit would aide in altitude sickness. Russell Colley made additions to the suit that enabled the first NASA astronauts to wear it.

42) Myra Maybelle Shirley Reed Starr was known as Belle Starr. She was a notorious Oklahoma outlaw accused of a number of crimes, mostly stealing horses. It was later realized that she did not actually commit these crimes, she only associated with criminals who did. She was also known to harbor outlaws, like the James brothers and the Youngers. In her late 30's she turned her life around and no longer associated with criminals. She was shot and killed two days before her 41st birthday. She was on her way home from a dance when she was ambushed, then shot and killed with her own rifle. It was said that she was murdered by a man who she turned down at the dance. There is a statue of Belle Starr outside the Woolaroc Museum. She is buried in an isolated grave in Porum, Oklahoma.

43) We are the childhood home to lots of actors! Here are just some of them.

Gene Autry, actor, museum, baseball team owner
Will Rogers
Nicki Aycox (Supernatural)
William Boyd (Hopalong Cassidy)
Darla Hood (Our Gang)
Ron Howard (Happy Days)
James Garner (The Notebook)
Rue McClanahan (Golden Girls)
Tony Randall (Odd Couple)
Dennis Weaver (Gunsmoke)
James Marsden (X Files)
Heather Langencamp (Nightmare on Elm Street)
Danny Cooksey (Diff'rent Strokes)
Chuck Norris (Walker, Texas Ranger)
Cindy Pickett (Ferris Bueller's Day Off)
Brad Pitt (Fight Club)
Lauren Stamile (Grey's Anatomy)

44) There was a Bigfoot sighting in Vici, Oklahoma in 1977. The town even sent out a search party. Nothing was found but we are still believers. (Most of us!)

45) Oklahoma is one of three states that produce helium.

46) A number of Oklahomans made their mark in the history of sports. These are a few.

Johnny Bench (Baseball Hall of Fame)
Willie Stargell (Pittsburgh Pirates)
Allie Reynolds (Cleveland Indians and New York Yankees)
Bobby Murcer (New York Yankees)
Lance Adams (Atlanta Braves)
Ryan Budde (Arizona Diamondbacks)
Nick Cole (Philadelphia Eagles)
Maurkice Pouncey (Pittsburgh Steelers)
Bud Wilkinson (Oklahoma University coach, College Football Hall of Fame)
Lance Norick (NASCAR)
Jim Ross (WWE Announcer)
Jerry Brisco (Wrestler)
Charlie Haas (WWE Wrestler)
Louise Brough (Hall of Fame Tennis Player)
Mikey Burnett (UFC Fighter)
Betty Jameson (Golf, World Golf Hall of Fame)
Charles Coe (Golf, winner of seven titles)
"Jumping Jack" McKracken (Basketball Hall of Fame)
Daniel Orton (Orlando Magic)
Tommy Morrison (Heavyweight Champion Boxer)
Shannon Miller (Gold Medal Gymnast winner)
Bart Conner (Two-time Gold Medal Gymnast winner)

46 Laws You Might be Breaking in Oklahoma

1) It is against the law to spit on a sidewalk.

2) In Clinton, it is illegal to molest an automobile.

3) It is illegal to carry tissues in the back of cars.

4) You can be fined or jailed for making an ugly face at a dog.

5) In Bartlesville, it is illegal to own more than two adult cats.

6) It is a misdemeanor to make noise in church.

7) It is illegal to say any curse words. If you get caught, that could be a $1 fine.

8) In Tulsa, you can not open a soda bottle without the supervision of a licensed engineer.

9) Women may not gamble in the nude, in lingerie, or while wearing a towel in Schulter.

10) In Bristow, Oklahoma it is against the law to serve water to a customer in a restaurant unless one peanut in a shell is also served. You can be fined up to $5 or violating this law.

11) It is illegal to play catch in the streets of Bartlesville.

12) It is illegal to wear a New York Jets jersey in Ada.

13) It is unlawful to put any hypnotized person in a display window in Hawthorne.

14) One may not promote a "horse tripping event."

15) It is against the law to take a bite out of another person's hamburger.

16) It is illegal for the owner of a bar to allow anyone inside to pretend to have sex with a buffalo.

17) Females are forbidden from doing their own hair without being licensed by the state.

18) Dogs must have a permit signed by the mayor in order to congregate in groups of three or more on private property.

19) It is illegal to buy a car on a Sunday. A 1959 law says selling, trading or bartering a car on Sunday is forbidden.

20) It is against the law to read a comic book while operating a motor vehicle.

21) It is illegal to wear your boots to bed.

22) It is illegal to have the hind legs of farm animals in your boots.

23) In Tulsa, it is illegal to boil, heat, or dry skunks or other wild animals with an offensive odor.

24) Cars must be tethered outside of public buildings.

25) Anyone arrested for soliciting a hooker must have their name and picture shown on television.

26) It is a $25 fine to call a female a slut, whore, or anything of the sort.

27) It is against the law to intentionally eavesdrop. If you repeat it and then publish it, you are guilty of a misdemeanor.

28) It is illegal to publish a lie in the newspaper.

29) One may not tip over a casket at a funeral in Oklahoma City.

30) In Bartelsville, if you run over someone's dog, you are legally obligated to pay for the dog's disposal.

31) Fish may not be contained in fishbowls on a public bus.

32) It is illegal to engage in, aide, or promote any animal gaming or racing of animals.

33) In Oklahoma City, it is illegal to own a stink bomb.

34) Whaling is illegal in the state of Oklahoma.

35) In Yukon, it is illegal to pass another vehicle without honking your horn.

36) It is illegal to walk backward while eating a hamburger in downtown Oklahoma City.

37) In Wynona, clothes may not be washed in a bird bath.

38) It is illegal to seduce a virgin by promising to marry her.

39) Mules may not drink out of bird baths in Wynona.

40) It is illegal to tie a horse in front of city hall.

41) In Seminole, it is illegal to sell mixed drinks on Labor Day.

42) It is a misdemeanor to ever use blasphemy. That includes words against Jesus, the Bible or anything under the cross.

43) It is also illegal to cause "annoying vibrations" in the city limits of Bartlesville. This includes loud music.

44) In Schulter, it is illegal for women to gamble in the nude, in lingerie, or in a towel.

45) Elephants are not to be taken into the downtown area of Tulsa.

46) You can get a $1,000 fine and jail time if you touch someone's glasses, hearing aid, or any "assistive device." This includes anything used to communicate, see, hear or maneuver.

46 Trips for Your Oklahoma Bucket List

1) Every year, Rush Springs, Oklahoma, holds an annual watermelon festival that includes a watermelon seed spitting contest, live entertainment, stage shows, a classic automotive show, electing a Watermelon Queen and loads of fresh watermelon to snack on. Driving home visitors are enticed by dozens of vendors set up along the highway selling their watermelons. This has to be the juiciest way to welcome summer!

2) The Red Earth Festival is held every year at the Cox Convention Center in downtown Oklahoma City. The event celebrates different Native American cultures. The events include a parade, dancing, a Pow Wow, and an art market. The festival now extends from the Convention Center to the Myriad Botanical Gardens. Art showcased and sold includes beadwork, basketry, jewelry, pottery, sculpture, paintings, graphics and cultural items.

3) Turner Falls Park, in Davis, is the oldest park in Oklahoma. Springs cascade down the Arbuckle Mountains into Honey Creek forming a natural swimming pool. Families across the country travel to swim in Honey Creek.

4) The Cherokee National Supreme Court Museum, in Tahlequah, is a combination of the history of the Cherokee judicial system and the Cherokee language celebrated in the field of Journalism. This includes an original printing press used by the Cherokee Advocate, a publication of the Cherokee nation and Oklahoma's first newspaper.

5) The National Cowboy & Western Heritage Museum in Oklahoma City is dedicated to the life and the heritage of the American cowboy. The museum includes western art, interactive galleries, Victorian firearms, and the National

Cowboy Hall of Fame. Activities at the museum include their popular Chuck Wagon Gathering & Children's Cowboy Festival that hosts an Old West show, covered wagon rides, authentic chuckwagon food and so much more.

6) In downtown Oklahoma, you can stand in the "Center of the Universe." It is best described as a "little-known mysterious acoustic phenomenon." The Center of the Universe is a small concrete circle in the middle of a larger circle of bricks. "If you stand in the middle of the circle and make a noise, the sound is echoed back several times louder than it was made." But none of the sounds can be heard from outside of the circle.

7) The annual Prague Kolache Festival celebrates the Czech heritage of Prague. Dance to polka music, enjoy a variety of delicious food and admire the Czech costumes. There is so much to enjoy throughout the day including a parade, beer garden, wine tasting booths, pony rides, a mechanical bull, carnival booths, and much more entertainment.

8) The Ponca City Herb Festival is a celebration dedicated to nature! The festival is host to more than 100 vendors showcasing plants, birdhouses, yard and garden ornaments, herbal vinegar and oils, herbal teas, and more. There is also a selection of quilts, handmade baskets, candles, soaps, bath products, furniture, and stoneware. There are seminars and group discussions on growing and using herbs, garden recipes, landscaping techniques, and information on wildflowers and roses and landscaping. Admission to the Herb Festival is free!

9) Every year the Oklahoma Historical Society hosts a Civil War Reenactment. They rotate the event among the Battle of Middle Boggy (in Allen), the Battle of Honey Springs (in Checotah), and the Battle of Cabin Creek (in Big Cabin).

10) Center of the Universe Festival is a music festival held in downtown Tulsa. Approximately 80,000 people attend the music event every July.

11) Dusk 'Til Dawn Blues Festival is a 3-day event celebrating Blues music. It is held in Rentiesville, the birthplace of blues musician, D.C. Minner.

12) If you are a fan of action figures then the Toy & Action Figure Museum will be your happy place. The museum boasts action figures of superheroes, the Simpsons, army men, Disney, and so much more. It was the first museum showcasing action figures and has visitors from across America and 40 other countries.

13) Sandhills Curiosity Shop is a unique market located on the famous Route 66. Harley and Annabelle Russell opened the shop. They call themselves Mediocre Music Makers. They enjoy playing music for each other and everyone that stops by to shop or just to visit.

14) The Overholser Mansion is a home decorated to reflect life in the early 1900's. Most of the furniture inside was owned by members of the Overholser family. Henry Overholser is considered to be the Father of Oklahoma City. His family home is now a hot tourist spot in Oklahoma City.

15) The Centennial Plaza in Ponca City shows a history of Oklahoma. The centered building has an architecture of the Spanish colonial forces. It was dedicated during the 100th anniversary of the Land Run of 1889. The ground is decorated with 6,527 bricks with family names engraved on them. The Daughters of the American Revolution added a memorial fountain and a War Memorial tablet dedicated to men and women who served in World War 1. There is also Fire Station #1 (a Spanish designed building), and three statues at the Plaza. They are of Lew Wentz and Ernest

Whitworth Marland (a former Congressman and Oklahoma governor). The third is a statue titled the Centennial Monument and symbolizes the men who participated in the Land Run.

16) Take a sight-seeing tour on the Cherokee Queen Riverboat Ride in Grand Lake, Oklahoma. The boat travels from Sailboat Bridge to Monkey Island.

17) Ed Galloway's Totem Pole Park was constructed by Ed Galloway. He was once a manual arts teacher at the Children's Home orphanage in Sand Springs, Oklahoma. Inside the park is an 11-sided Fiddle House, with totem poles inside and out. The house also has hand carved fiddles, handmade furniture, and portraits of each US President up to John Kennedy. There are four smaller totem poles around the park, along with, picnic tables, barbecues, animal-form seats and animal-form gateposts. Their main attraction is the world's largest concrete totem pole. It is 90 feet tall and is decorated with 200 images of Native American portraits, symbols, and animals.

18) The Pecan Festival held every June, in Okmulgee, holds claim to the world record for the largest pecan pie, pecan cookie, pecan brownie, and biggest ice cream and cookie party. Children go nuts over their mascot, Squiggy, the Pecan loving squirrel. There is a barbecue competition, along with, vendors and food booths that include lots of pecan treats. For those who love to bake there is a Cookie Contest! The most important rule to enter the contest is that at least 1 cup of pecans are used in the recipe. They even hold a Pet Parade that features animals of all types. There are a variety of categories that give these pet lovers a chance to earn a ribbon.

19) The McLoud Blackberry Festival is a 2-day event that celebrates everything blackberries. Along with fresh

blackberries, there is the blackberry flavored cobbler, sodas, and teas. Events include a parade, live entertainment, a pageant, fireworks and more. There is even a blackberry pie eating contest. The event started in the 1940's to celebrate the end of harvest.

20) The Porter Peach festival was first held in 1967. The festival celebrates the Porter peaches, which are so popular in the state that only a small amount is sold outside of Oklahoma. The event held every July includes free peaches & ice cream, dessert and cooking contests featuring top-notch peach dishes, prize peach auctions, and the best peach cobbler you will ever taste.

21) The deadCenter Film Festival is fun for all types of movie lovers. They held their first festival in the year 2000 in downtown Oklahoma City. It was since named "one of the Top 20 Coolest Film Festivals in the World," by MovieMaker Magazine. The five-day event plays over 100 indie films from across the country. There are also workshops and movie parties to enjoy.

22) Tahlequah holds the Medicine Show, a 3-day celebration to Red Dirt music. Visitors can camp out at the concert site or bring chairs and blankets and spend the day.

23) Clinton's Water-Zoo Park is the best water park in the country. There is the Tiger Slide for toddlers and preschoolers, 3 twisted water slides for families that are different lengths, and the 4-story waterslides. One is a body-slide and two are tube-slides. Along with the waterslides, there is a splash pad, wave pool, and lazy river.

24) Pioneer Village is a step back in time to explore Oklahoma history, from the days of the Land Rush to the early development days of the state. The Village includes the Original Kingfisher Bank, the Gant School House, Harmony

Church, a Jail Cell, Dalton Cabin, Cole Cabin, Cook Shack, a Blacksmith Shop, and even an Outhouse.

25) The USS Batfish is located at the Muskogee War Memorial Park. The USS Batfish sank 15 vessels during World War II. An accomplishment that no other submarine has reached. The submarine was moved from Texas to Oklahoma and is open for tours. When you walk through the submarine you can almost feel the tense days lived by the Navy soldiers that once commanded the USS Batfish.

26) The Myriad Gardens in Oklahoma City is one of the most beautiful sites home to Oklahoma. The Botanical Gardens is gorgeous inside and out. This includes ornamental gardens, a children's garden, a lake, an off-leash dog park, splash fountains for children, and outdoor trails. During the summer they host the Children's Garden Festival where they transfer the garden into a storybook/cartoon character's world. They hold a variety of activities for the day. Be sure to watch their website for listings of events they hold all year. Just some of these are Twilight Concerts on the Great Lawn, painting, crafts, activities built around storybook and a popular Internet Cat Video Festival hosted by Midtown Vets.

27) Everyone should see the all-wooden carousel in Ackley Park. The carousel has 36 hand-carved horses and two chariots. It is a must see!

28) If you love hard rock then you will love Rocklahoma. This is a 3-day hard rock music festival held in Pryor, Oklahoma. Spend the day listening to music or campout and enjoy the events from start to finish.

29) Gandini's Circus is nestled in the grassy lands of Edmond, Oklahoma. Walk around the array of trailers and cages and explore an abandoned part of Oklahoma history.

30) Will Rogers Park is a 30-acre park. Seven of those acres is an entire rose garden. The finishing touch to the park is an 8-foot high waterfall that cascades into East Lake.

31) Oklahoma honors their Native American history and if you want to hear more about it from the Native Americans themselves then you will want to join in the Stories on the Square event, held at Cherokee National Capitol in Tahlequah. Storytellers will fill you with stories of American Indian heritage and culture. When the stories come to an end, children are invited to make a special craft at the Cherokee National Prison Museum.

32) Some time in the 60's a cement truck wrecked in Winganon. The truck rolled over on its side. The company came to retrieve the truck but they left behind the mixer behind because it was full and too difficult to get off the ground. Through the years residents decorated to look like a piece of a NASA shuttle. It's become a popular landmark. Do you want to see it? The cement mixer is located along Winganon Road between Highway 169 and Oologah Lake.

33) The Oklahoma Frontier Drugstore Museum, in Guthrie, preserves the history of pharmacy and medical health professionals in the state of Oklahoma. The museum also includes an old-fashioned soda fountain and the Oklahoma Pharmacy Heritage Foundation Hall of Fame. They opened in 1992. In 2006 they added an Apothecary Garden. They are located inside the Gaffney building that was built in 1890.

34) Visit Spiro Mounds Archaeological Park! They discovered that Native Americans lived on the site between 850 A.D. to 1450 A.D. The 150 acres include exhibits and a one-half mile trail. They have guided tours and planned events throughout the year.

35) Honobia hosts an Annual Bigfoot Festival and

Conference the first Friday and Saturday, every October. The area was selected because they have had the most Bigfoot sightings and encounters. The festival celebrates everything Bigfoot, including live entertainment and storytelling. Throughout the rest of the year, the Honobia Bigfoot Organization works hard raising money to provide scholarships to students surrounding the Honobia area.

36) Did you know that the Twister movie was filmed in Oklahoma? Explore the Twister Museum in Wakita and check out the movie props, memorabilia, and behind-the-scenes videos. On your way into town, you can have your photo taken at the water tower that was featured in the movie. When you plan your trip here remember that it is only open April through September.

37) Frontier City is a Wild West amusement park first built in 1958 in Oklahoma City. When the park first opened, in lieu of a ribbon-cutting ceremony, a six-shooter aimed at a piece of rope. A similar event still takes place at the start of each day.

38) Good things come in small packages at Flames to Hope in Noble, Oklahoma. You will fall in love with horses in a whole new way when you explore the home of the country's most adorable miniature horses. Families from across the state bring their mini ponies to compete in the mini cart driving obstacle course and mini talent show. The ponies also help people who have suffered trauma and those in physical and occupational therapy.

39) The Paradise Alley Food Truck Park in Ardmore is a must-stop picnic place to have lunch. They have events throughout the year and sometimes even live entertainment. Good food and good family fun!

40) Visit Black Mesa Park to walk along the dinosaur tracks. You read that correctly, the dinosaur tracks were discovered

in the 1980s. The tracks can be found along the Carrizo Creek. In one point you can see where the dinosaurs slipped in the mud.

41) Reunion Days in Stigler is an event like no other. Enjoy a gospel music festival, along with turtle races, horseshoe contests, and even a bubble gum blowing contest.

42) Do you have a thing for skeletons and skulls? Then you have something in common with Jay Villemarette, founder of the Museum of Osteology in Oklahoma City. The museum houses hundreds of skeletons and skulls. There are also educational programs for students that teach the purpose and role of the skeleton in animals and people.

43) At the Tulsa Balloon Festival, you can see a variety of colorful hot air balloons that provide twice-daily flights. The balloons will light up the sky at the end of the day. Enjoy the carnival while you soak in the beauty of the hot air balloons.

44) Are you looking for something spooky? Well, Oklahoma has their share of haunted havens. There is the Bird Creek School in Pawhuska. This is a one-room schoolhouse from the early 1900's that was built for Native American children. It is said that if you write your name on the chalkboard and leave for a few minutes; when you return it will be erased. If you travel to the Mohawk Park & Gold Course, it is said to be haunted across the whole property and mostly in the Gold facility. The oddest report there is from those who claim the lights were on even though there is no electricity.

45) Still looking for something scary? You can find that in Guthrie at the Blue Belle Saloon. It was a bordello owned and run by Miss Lizzie and her girls Claudia and Estelle. Tragically, Claudia was found beaten to death. Shortly after that Miss Lizzie and Estelle both died from unknown causes. Miss Lizzie and Claudia are buried inside the saloon. It is

believed that all three girls haunt the saloon today, along with a man with a handlebar mustache. Upstairs of the salon are the rooms where the bordello was operated. People often report hearing moans, crying, pounding, singing, and voices talking. Miss Lizzie was thought to be a Christian even though she hired young girls to work in her brothel. Some families sold their daughters to her for use in the brothel.

46) A Sad Papaw Cookout! No Bucket List is complete without spending an afternoon at a Sad Papaw cookout. The Sad Papaw tweet sent out on March 16, 2016, has grown into a movement to acknowledge our grandparents and the benefits of connecting whenever possible. Our grandparents are the matriarchs of our families. Never miss an opportunity to pop in for a visit and reconnect. You can also follow Sad Papaw's book signing events on his Facebook page.

46 Reasons to Love Oklahoma

1) We have a life-size statue of a cattle drive, titled "On the Chisholm Trail." It was placed in Duncan as a monument to the American Cowboy.

2) We have been the setting for some of the best movies, including Twister, Rain Man, The Outsiders, Near Dark, Phenomenon, The Frighteners, Elizabethtown, Dillinger, Splinter, and All-American Murder.

3) We have teepees that you can spend the night in at Roman Nose State Park. Spend days swimming, fishing, hiking, riding horses, walking the trails or out on the paddle boats. Nothing tops sleeping in an actual teepee.

4) We have 200 man-made lakes. More than any state in America.

5) We have a state fossil, the Saurophaganax Maximus. It is a species of Allosaurus that roamed the state of Oklahoma 151 million years ago. You can also see the Oklahoma State Dinosaur, Acrocanthosaurus atokensis, at the Museum of the Red River in Idabel.

6) We have the longest stretch of Route 66 running through Oklahoma. When traveling the road, you must stop and check-out the Tally's Good Food Cafe. Tally's opened on Friday the 13th, in November 1937. Since the year they opened, they have served free Thanksgiving meals to the homeless.

7) We have the Black Mesa State Park, a stargazing hot spot! The Okie-Tex Star Party is an eight-night stargazing event that includes speakers, food, and giveaways.

8) We have Danny Hodge, who was born and raised in Perry, Oklahoma. He still lives there today! Hodge is considered one of the greatest wrestlers of all time. He is the only amateur wrestler to be on the cover of Sport's Illustrated. He won the silver medal in the 1956 Olympics and is the only amateur wrestler to be on the cover of Sport's Illustrated.

9) We have green and white as our state colors. Psychologists believe that the color green relaxes the body. This is why talk shows have "Green Rooms." The color green also improves reading and creativity.

10) We have an official state meal: Fried okra, squash, cornbread, barbecue pork, biscuits, sausage & gravy, grits, corn, strawberries, chicken-fried steak, pecan pie, black-eyed peas, adopted in 1988.

11) We have the Arcadia Round Barn located on Highway 66, east of Edmond. It's been an Oklahoma landmark for nearly 20 years.

12) We have gorgeous scenery, wide open prairies, and even 51 parks! Get your camera ready!

13) We have the Blue Whale of Catoosa, located on Route 66, the whale has greeted visitors since 1972. Hugh Davis built the whale as a gift for his wife's on their 34th wedding anniversary. Take a walk through the whale's mouth and come out to a diving dock for a swim in the pond....or sit on the edge, kick your feet and soak in the sun.

14) We have been named the "buckle of the Bible belt." The oldest church, still open today, is the Baptist Mission Church, in Adair County which was formed in 1830.

15) We have a statue of the giant praying hands outside Oral

Roberts University in Tulsa. Do you remember those famous praying hands seen on prints, journal covers, etched in glass, and more?

16) We have a heart for all types of music that we celebrate with a variety of museums and festivals These are just a few musicians that call Oklahoma home:

Hoyt Axton (Never Been to Spain)
Hanson (Mmm Bop)
Elvin Bishop (Fooled Around and Fell in Love)
Bob Bogle (The Ventures)
Garth Brooks
Toby Keith
Mel McDaniel
Reba McEntire
Leona Mitchell (Oklahoma Music Hall of Fame)
Gary Chapman (Christian Musician)
Charlie Christian (Jazz musician, Rock & Roll Hall of Fame)
Ronnie Dunn (half of Brooks and Dunn)
David Gates (Bread)
Sheb Wooley (Purple People Eater)
B.J. Thomas (Raindrops Keep Fallin' On My Head)
Blake Shelton
Neal Schon (Journey)
Joe Don Rooney (part of Rascal Flatts)

17) We have the home where the buffalo roam. Bison can still be found in the Tallgrass Prairie Preserve, the Wichita National Wildlife Refuge, Woolaroc Ranch, and the Pawnee Bill Ranch.

18) We have the Bedlam Series! You are guaranteed to have a great time, whether you route for Oklahoma University (Sooners) or Oklahoma Statue University (Cowboys and Cowgirls).

19) We have a state flag that is decorated with Native American symbols. The blue background represents the blue flag carried by the Choctaw during the Civil War. The shield in the center is similar to the battle shield of an Osage Indian warrior, with the addition of a buffalo hide cover. The flag includes two symbols of peace; the peace pipe and an olive branch. The original state flag was red but they changed it after the fear of communism grew.

20) We have a great state motto - "Labor Omnia Vincit." It means "Labor conquers all things."

21) We have some of the most beautiful lakes in America including Lake Texoma, Lake Eufaula, Lake Hefner, and Broken Bow Lake.

22) We have amazing waterfalls too! There is the Beavers Bend Waterfall in Broken Bow, Buffalo Springs in Sulphor, Natural Falls in Colcord, Turner Falls in Davis, and Little Niagara at Travertine Falls in Sulphor.

23) We have the outline of a meat cleaver. Yes, our state is shaped like a meat cleaver. That is a pretty good symbol for us since we produce 3.22 billion pounds of beef every year.

24) We have an official state poem. It is "Howdy Folks" written by David Randolph Milsten in honor of the Will Rogers memorial dedication on November 4, 1938.

25) We have 39 American Indian tribes in our state today. There are 25 Native American languages still spoken here.

26) We have Robbers Cave State Park that was used by early outlaws, like Jesse James and Belle Star, to hide from the law. Along with the caves, the park boasts 8,000 acres of rugged land and three lakes.

27) We have the Scissor-Tailed Flycatcher as our state bird. The bird has a tail that is twice as long as its body. The tail resembles a pair of scissors, which is how it earned the name " Scissor-Tailed Flycatcher."

28) We have the Will Rogers World Airport. It is one of the busiest airports in Oklahoma. Even though it has "World" in the title, they do not offer international flights. Did you know that Will Rogers is one of the most famous entertainers from Oklahoma? He starred in 71 movies and wrote more than 4,000 newspaper columns.

29) We have the Indian Blanket as our state wildflower. The red and yellow wildflower blooms in June and July. In 2004, they made the Oklahoma Rose the state flower.

30) We have the Amateur Softball Association of America. The group was founded in 1933 and has grown into the strongest softball organization in the entire United States. We also have the National Softball Hall of Fame and Museum in Oklahoma City.

31) We have the Twin House in Oklahoma City. Four women that lived in the home, in consecutive years, gave birth to boy-girl twins.

32) We have the honor of declaring that we started the Girl Scout cookie craze! Girl Scout troop leader, Juliette Gordon Low, in Muskogee, first sold the cookies as a service project. They were sugar cookies made by scratch by her troop.

33) We have the Oklahoma City Land Run Monument featuring 45 bronze statues made in the image of early Oklahomans.

34) We have a state song, It is "Oklahoma," written by Oscar Hammerstein in 1943.

35) We have towns like Okay, Slaughterville, Frogville, Hooker, Slapout, Cookietown, and Bushy Head. By the way, Cookietown was named after Mercantile Owner, Marvin Cornelius, who was known to always have cookies to pass out to the children.

36) We have Shamen's Portal, also known as Beaver Sands Portal, in Beaver's Dune State Park. It is believed to have caused a number of mysterious deaths. Legend has it that there is a flash of green light before the person disappears.

37) We have more tornadoes than any state in America. It's a Storm Chaser's dream!

38) We have Milk Bottle Grocery in Oklahoma City. There is a giant milk bottle hoisted on top. Milk Bottle Grocery was built in the 1920's and has been made a historic landmark.

39) We have the OETA Movie Club. The PBS affiliate channel is home to the movie club that plays classic films from 1930 until 1970. There was an exception to the timeline when they played "Julie and Julia." They selected the movie as a tribute to Julia Childs who once worked with PBS. Jeff Morava produces and directs the selected films while Robert Burch hosts the event. During intermissions, Burch fills viewers with fun facts about the movie and what was going on in the world when the film was made. In February 1988, the Movie Club celebrated its 30th anniversary. They brought back BJ Wexler, the show's original host to commemorate the success of the OETA Movie Club.

40) We have Maysville, the home of Charles Burford. He is the farmer that saved your bread from going stale! That's right, the twist tie on bread bags was his creation.

41) We have Pops, a restaurant located on Route 66. They sell 100's of different flavors of soda pop. They are arranged

by color. The crowning jewel of Pops is a 66-foot tall neon-colored soda pop bottle outside. There are over 600 flavors of pop sold there. Just some of those fun flavors are cherry, watermelon, bacon, cream corn, coffee, and chocolate.

42) We have the Hopes and Dreams statue in downtown Perry. The statue was crafted in the image of a pioneer couple. It was placed on a massive granite pedestal as a Cherokee Strip Centennial memorial. On the back of the pedestal are the names of frontiersmen and boomers.

43) We have our own Holy City located in the Wichita Mountains. The 66 acres was modeled to resemble what Israel looked like during Biblical times. They hold a show titled, The Prince of Peace, which is America's longest running Easter play.

44) We have a haunted hotel. The Stone Lion Inn is a Victorian Mansion built in 1907. FE Houghton and his wife had the home built for their 12 children. Their daughter, August had fallen ill with whooping cough. She was mistakenly given the wrong dosage of medicine and died. Sometime after that, for a period of 8 years, a local undertaker rented a space in the home to use as a mortuary. People who have stayed at the inn claim to have heard and seen the spirits of Houghton and August.

45) We have The Diner! This cozy restaurant in Norman earned its claim to fame by being featured twice on the Food Network. The Diner was shown on "Diners, Drive-Ins and Dives" and on "American Diner Revival."

46) We have Sad Papaw! The tweet sent out by his granddaughter Kelsey started a movement across the country to remind people, to never forget to spend time with your grandparents.

Coming in March 2019...
Sad Papaw 1968